Amazing Tales
of the
Old West

Jeff O'Donnell

Dageforde Publishing

ISBN: 1-886225-17-6
Library of Congress Catalog Card Number: 96-70909

Cover Art by Angie Johnson Art Productions

Dageforde Publishing
941 'O' Street, Suite 728
Lincoln, Nebraska 68508-3625
(402) 475-1123 FAX (402) 475-1176
e-mail: dageforde.lnk@ispi.net
www.dageforde.com

Dedicated

To my wife Cindy with all my love

Table of Contents

A "Withdrawal" from the Treasury

On the afternoon of February 28, 1885, the occupants of the Nebraska state offices, members of the legislature, and any visitors who happened to be in the state capitol building were startled by two loud shots fired in rapid succession. The shots seemed to come from the hallway on the first floor of the west wing. Confusion reigned as people ran up and down the hallways, all wondering what was happening. It would be only a short time before it became clear that someone had been shot and serious events were occurring.

The two shots signaled the beginning of one of the most bizarre robbery attempts in the history of the Old West. No one would have suspected that the unlikely looking trio of men who had entered the Nebraska State Treasury office that cold winter afternoon were intent on robbing the treasury in broad daylight. One of the men hobbled along on a wooden leg, another was unarmed, and the third would later be accused of informing on the other two. Incredibly, they had only one very old, tired horse to use for their getaway. The men did not even

1

seem concerned that they had chosen to rob the treasury at the busiest time of the day with the legislature in session and visitors continually coming and going.

This strange attempted robbery threw the fast-growing prairie city of Lincoln, Nebraska, into an uproar. Even though the townspeople considered themselves quite civilized, they were reminded that the Old West was still very much alive in 1885. Rumors soon spread that the robbery was a farce initiated by Governor James Dawes in order to enhance his own political image. Unfortunately, one man was shot and killed, and another went on trial for his life as an aftermath of the events that took place that day.

At 2:00 p.m., three rough-looking men walked into the Nebraska State Treasury office on the first floor of the capitol building. When all three had entered the office, bandit Alvin McGuire, a man who had been in and out of jail many times in the past, turned and tried to lock the door behind him. Although the lock would not work, Charles Daly and James Griffin, the other two bandits, walked up to the counter window and pulled pistols from beneath their coats. Pointing the guns at Deputy Treasurer G.M. Bartlett's head, they ordered, "Throw up your hands!"

A surprised Bartlett replied, "What does this mean, men? Is this fooling or business?"

"No talk," one of the robbers answered. "Hand out the money and be quick about it."

Bartlett quickly shoved a tray with three to four hundred dollars worth of gold coins through the opening of his window. Griffin dumped the booty into the pockets of his large overcoat. Daly kept his gun trained on Bartlett while the other two men backed slowly out of the office and into the hallway.

Suddenly two shots rang out, echoing up and down the hallway. The acrid smell of gunpowder filled the capitol's first floor as people in the hallway headed for cover. Daly slammed the treasury door shut and ran behind the counter where Bartlett stood, opened the window, and leaped out. A detective hiding in a cellar just below the window took a shot at McGuire and Griffin, but Daly made good on his escape.

Detective Alva Pound ordered the two of them to halt, but they ignored the command and ran for the capitol's front entrance as fast as they could go. As Detective Pound yelled for Griffin, the peg-legged bandit, to stop, McGuire quickly raised his hands high above his head and stopped running. Griffin, however, looking over his shoulder, raised his arm and waved his pistol in what Pound thought to be a threatening manner. Pound would later testify that at that moment, he heard a snap which he thought to be the hammer of Griffin's pistol falling onto a cartridge. Raising his shotgun, Pound pulled both triggers, riddling the unfortunate Griffin with over seventy balls of double B buckshot. Pound quickly arrested McGuire.

Griffin lay on the floor, blood gushing from wounds in his right side. The unconscious bandit was carried to the basement of the capitol, where a doctor tried to save his life. The doctor could do nothing for him, and the terrible wound proved fatal. Griffin died after two hours, never regaining consciousness.

As soon as the senate had sufficiently recovered from the excitement to proceed with business, Governor Dawes sent a communication calling attention to the

*The State Capitol in Lincoln, Nebraska, was the scene of one of the
Old West's most unusual holdup attempts.*
(Nebraska State Historical Society)

services rendered by the detectives in protecting the
state treasury. The communication was referred to the
Committee on Ways and Means, which immediately
added an amendment to an appropriation bill giving
$500 each to detectives Pound, Davis, and Thompson.

Before the day had ended, rumor and hearsay began to swirl around the day's events. Daly's easy escape
through the window threw suspicion on Pound. "Was
the killing of Griffin justified?" became common talk. Reporters wanted to know why Detective Pound happened
to be waiting conveniently outside the treasury office's
door. Where was Daly? Why was there only one getaway horse?

4

In scenes reminiscent of present-day Watergate and Irangate, reporters from all three Lincoln newspapers wanted answers to those questions. To make matters worse, the coroner's inquest on Griffin was kept secret. The detectives had wanted a public inquest so they could be exonerated of any suspicion of collusion on their part, but the coroner countered by saying secrecy had been imposed to prevent publication of any evidence before McGuire's impending trial.

In order to quell the rumors and explain what had happened, Detective Pound was forced to hold an early-day press conference. Pound's story was backed up by Governor Dawes, who, no doubt by then, saw big trouble looming in his political future and had agreed it was time to tell the public the whole story.

Daly, the robber who escaped through the window, had come to Pound with the story of the robbery plot two weeks before the holdup took place. Pound, in turn, consulted with Dawes who encouraged him to let the plot mature. Both men decided to set a trap for the would-be bandits and arrest them after they robbed the treasury.

Pound carefully placed one officer in the basement to guard the back window of the treasury office. He stationed another detective in the vault room of the treasury office; from there the detective could signal when the robbers had entered the office. Pound himself took a stand in the treasury office's back room by a door leading to the hallway corridor.

When the robbers arrived and entered the office, Pound's assistant quickly signaled. The detective stepped into the hallway and waited by the treasury door for the bandits to emerge. Pound thought it would be easy to arrest the surprised robbers, and everything went according to plan until Griffin refused to stop and turned to threaten Pound with his pistol. When Pound saw Griffin point the gun at him and heard the hammer click, he panicked and fired both barrels of his shotgun in self-defense.

Pound also admitted to reporters that his detectives apprehended Daly later on the day of the attempted robbery. It was openly speculated that Daly was kept under wraps to enhance- the detectives' reputation as lawmen in the highest degree.

The coroner's inquest was held March 1, 1885. It revealed that Griffin's pistol was loaded at the time of his death. It also confirmed there was an indentation on one of the cartridges, proving Griffin had indeed pulled the trigger as Pound testified.

Up to the time of the inquest, public sentiment favored the two criminals, McGuire and Daly. Even with the results of the inquest made public, people wanted to hang Pound from the nearest tree for shooting a "poor, innocent, one-legged, harmless bandit." The house defeated the proposal to reward Pound and his detectives, and the money was deleted from the appropriations bill of Nebraska's 19th Legislature.

Indicted for robbery, McGuire was tried in District Court in Lincoln. His attorneys based their case on the fact that Pound's detectives had gotten McGuire drunk and lured him into the commission of the crime. That revelation hardly enhanced the reputations of Governor Dawes and Detective Pound. Not surprisingly to anyone who followed the trial, McGuire was acquitted after the jury deliberated three short hours.

Charles Daly was also indicted for the robbery; however, the results of his trial are a mystery for no public record on its outcome can be located. It can be assumed, however, that he was likely acquitted, given the mood of the public. He was never heard of again.

Things were not quite so easy for Pound. With public sentiment running high against him, he was indicted for murder in the second degree and tried in Lincoln's District Court eight months later. Pound testified that he shot Griffin in self-defense, to protect others in the hallway and to prevent his escape. His lawyers also claimed he was only doing his duty as a peace officer.

The prosecuting attorney, however, claimed that Pound shot Griffin without giving him the opportunity to surrender. A second motive for the shooting was introduced when J.H. Brown took the stand. Brown, a former justice of the peace, testified that a year earlier Griffin had talked to him on the street saying, "The general public has more respect for me now than they have had for some time. Why don't you say good morning?"

Brown noticed a large, sharp knife clutched in Griffin's hand and replied, "Griffin, I have no business with you."

"I have no particular complaint against you," Griffin replied. "You have put me in jail two or three times, but I want you to beware whom you send after me." Griffin did not mention any names to Brown, but he did say he would never let a certain man in town take him into custody alive. Brown took this man to be Pound.

The jury deliberated for twelve hours before reaching a verdict. They found Pound guilty of manslaughter and recommended him to the mercy of the court. He was sentenced to two years in the federal penitentiary;

Governor James W. Dawes' political career was permanently damaged by his involvement with the attempted robbery of the state treasury.
(Nebraska State Historical Society)

however, upon hearing the sentence, the district attorney said that although he prosecuted the case to its fullest, he did not feel Pound was a bad character. McGuire was tried and acquitted, and because he had gone free, the district attorney felt Pound should also be set free.

A petition asking Governor Dawes to pardon Pound was quickly circulated. On receiving the petition, Dawes promptly pardoned and freed the grateful Pound.

In sorting out this strange event, it appears that the only person who did not know what was going on was poor Griffin. McGuire and Daly both testified that Pound and Dawes had coerced them into going on with the robbery. Given J. L. Brown's testimony, it also appears that some event in the past had created bad blood between Pound and Griffin. One could make the case that Griffin was not only set up by McGuire and Daly, but by Pound as well.

While Pound's part in the mess was probably both to satisfy a personal grievance and to enhance his reputation as a good detective, Governor Dawe's involvement was purely political. He, no doubt, felt that foiling a robbery of the Nebraska State Treasury would further his career.

Detective Pound would be dogged the rest of his days by the actions he took during the whole sordid affair. Governor James Dawes would survive politically, but his reputation would always remain tarnished by his role in the robbery that really wasn't.

The Lynching of Elizabeth Taylor
Murder or Justice?

Late in the evening of March 14, 1885, some fifty grim-faced, determined men gathered in a field beside a bridge four-and-a-half miles east and south of the Oregon Trail that cut through southwestern Clay County, Nebraska. There, in the pale moonlight, the armed and angry men quickly crossed the bridge, made a sharp turn off the road, and descended the opposite river bank. They were headed for a sod house about a hundred yards from a bridge that crossed the Blue River.

By prearranged signal, several of the men covered the two windows in the sod house while the rest of the group half-circled around to the front door. One of them called out and demanded the hasty exit of the occupants. No one answered. After several angry requests and a threat to toss dynamite down the chimney, there was a sudden flurry of activity within the soddy.

Slowly the door opened and five hired hands — "Texas Bill" Foster, Nelson Cellery, N.C. Clark, a man called "Farrell," and a young lad named Luther Wiggins — came out. They were quickly searched, tied, bound,

The last to leave the soddy were a man, warmly clothed, and a woman clad only in a nightgown. Both were grabbed and dragged from the soddy. (Illustrations by Mick Harrison)

and placed under guard. The last to leave the soddy were a man, warmly clothed, and a woman clad only in a nightgown. Both were grabbed and dragged from the soddy. The man offered little resistance, while the woman struggled, insisting she be allowed to return to the soddy and get decently clothed. One of the men brought a shawl from the soddy and threw it around her shoulders before her arms were tied to her body.

The vigilantes forced the two victims along the bank, up the road, away from the bridge and to a field two furlongs from the sod house. There, the men held a trial, acting as prosecutor, judge, and jury. It's likely Elizabeth Taylor thought her sentence would be banishment from Clay County and, in order to end her discomfort, pleaded guilty to one of the crimes of which she stood accused; persuading her brother Thomas Jones to hire a man to burn down the neighbor's barn.

Her quick confession ended the mock trial. Quickly, the other prisoners were taken to the house of Rees T. Rees, one of the vigilantes, with orders that they be guarded closely. Elizabeth and Thomas were taken down the road to the sod house by the bridge. Neither realized that Elizabeth's confession would lead to their grisly demise. In fact, not until they stopped on the bridge and saw the men fashioning nooses out of several leather halters did they realize the fate that awaited them.

Thomas Jones pleaded first for both their lives, then for his sister's. The only answer he received was a warning to make peace with his Maker. Elizabeth gasped, cried out, and fell to her knees. Once again Thomas pleaded for mercy. Again his appeal was denied. Thomas then knelt awkwardly beside his sister. She raised her head and tried to stop her tears. After a moment, the doomed Welshman and his sister said the Lord's Prayer in their native tongue.

When their "amens" sounded, both of them were pulled roughly to their feet. Four men, two on either side of the prisoners, marched them from the center to the south side of the bridge where they were turned and forced to walk down the bank alongside the pilings into the cold, shallow water, to an oblong sandbar which extended an equal distance on either side of the bridge.

The nooses were lowered from the bridge and placed around their necks. Then the victims were forced to mount horses. They gradually ceased struggling as the nooses were pulled taut about their heads and the ends of the halters were tied to bridge stringers above them. At a blast of gunfire, the horses broke across the sandbar and away from the two struggling, twisting figures hanging from the bridge. The vigilantes remained silent until they were certain no sign of life remained in their victims' bodies. The mob released Taylor's five hired men, most of whom left the county.

What led to the first and only lynching of a woman in Nebraska history? What motivated those men to try, sentence, and execute her?

Elizabeth Taylor was an ambitious, determined woman. She was accused of several crimes, none of which were ever proved; however, circumstantial evidence and hateful innuendo made her a prime target for what happened that night along the Blue River.

On March 16, the editor of the *Hastings Gazette-Journal*, published in adjoining Adams County, promised his readers, "News reached this city yesterday that Mrs. Taylor and her brother Tom Jones had been lynched. It seems that the lynching took place about 2:00 a.m. Sunday morning. The victims were taken out and hanged to a bridge near their house. Our reporter has gone to the scene of the hanging of Mrs. Taylor and her brother Tom Jones so that we will have completest details possible."

Unfortunately, the "completest details" were never published. Readers were never informed about the dynamite threat, the trial in the field, Jones's plea for his sister's life, or their last-minute prayers.

Elizabeth Jones was twenty years old when she married James A. Taylor, son of Mrs. Martha Taylor of Lookout, Pettis Point, Missouri. Elizabeth and James left Missouri shortly after the birth of their first son, William, in 1872. They moved to Clay County, Nebraska, where, on April 24, James filed for his first seventy-five acres near Spring Ranch Precinct. Elizabeth's father, John, and her brother Tom, moved to the precinct at the same time. Elizabeth soon gave birth to two more children, John and Maggie.

By the summer of 1880, with the influx of immigrants and landseekers from the east, the population of the precinct had grown considerably and numerous sod houses were built. During that time Elizabeth began having trouble with her neighbors.

Because of the heavily publicized trial of cattleman Print Oliver who was charged with murdering two homesteaders in Custer County, the settlers in Spring Ranch Precinct were more aware of their rights and privileges under Nebraska's herd law. When Taylor cattle, horses, or mules broke through the fence and wandered into fields, verbal apologies were no longer acceptable. Damages were cited, bills presented, and prompt restitution expected. Although James, Elizabeth, and their hired man Ben Bethlemer checked the fence on the three-quarter section ranch by day and tried to corral most of the stock by night, neighbors gave them little credit for their efforts.

Claims mounted, and while James paid, Elizabeth fumed. Her resentment turned to wrath. Because James had sold some stock on credit but then neglected to enforce the contracts when payments came due, she considered him weak and unwilling to stand up to the neighbors. What love and pride Elizabeth had for him turned to scorn.

To appease his wife, James deeded all their real and personal property to her in the late spring of 1881. That enabled Elizabeth to exercise rights granted under the Married Woman Property Act which made it possible for a female to buy, sell, or dispose of her property without her husband's consent. It wasn't long before every male in the precinct learned of the Taylors' highly irregular arrangement.

Before 1881 ended, James had lost every vestige of respect that his neighbors — especially the men — had for him, because he had made no effort to curb Elizabeth's activities and dealings. She made sure outstanding debts were collected, all livestock sales were made by written contract, and interest was added for credit with mortgages taken until payment was made. The men in Spring Ranch Precinct did not take kindly to being bested by a woman and soon grew to hate Elizabeth.

In the spring of 1882, James began to complain of feeling poorly and being troubled with stomach pains. If he had died in bed, or had consulted a doctor about his condition before his death on May 27, 1882, critics might have had sympathy for the widow. Instead, his sudden death only generated suspicions.

On a warm afternoon, a neighbor fishing on the Blue River saw James riding a horse like a "wildman" towards the river. The desperate man literally fell off his horse and began gulping water until, suddenly, he pitched face first into the river. By the time the neighbor reached him, James was dead.

People doubted the coroner's ruling of "death by natural causes" when they learned Elizabeth had purchased large amounts of potato-bug killer some months earlier. Because the Taylors had never been known to plant potatoes, suspicion blossomed that Elizabeth had intended to kill more than bugs.

James was barely cold in his grave before Rees T. Rees, a bachelor who lived across the road from the Taylors, started to pay calls on the widow. He was tall, dark, rather handsome, and two years her junior. His impatience and lack of tact in asking her to become his wife so soon after her husband's funeral aroused her suspicions. Finally, she told him she was not interested and sent him packing. From that moment, Elizabeth knew she had made a dangerous enemy.

Thomas Jones began to lose friends because of his loyalty to Elizabeth. He had successfully farmed the land he and his father jointly owned, and he had used part of his savings to make investments in Juniata, a small town west of Hastings. By spring 1883, he and his sister decided to pool land and resources for a joint stock operation. Like Elizabeth, Thomas could see more profit in livestock than in corn or wheat.

But they had a problem. Elizabeth was land and cattle poor; Thomas had little cash on hand, so they needed more help. Elizabeth solved an employee problem by leaving word at all the livestock dealers and livery stables in surrounding towns that tobacco, board, and bunk were available at the sod house on the Blue River for any man needing work. Soon, cowboy drifters learned they were welcome — no questions asked — for as long as they wanted to stay, provided they repaid hospitality with work.

In spite of the influx of migrants to the Spring Ranch Precinct, the combined livestock operation encountered little trouble. Neighboring landowners John Llewelyn, Rees, and Joseph Beyer, however, did make a point of checking fences during crop-growing and harvest times and informed new neighbors of their rights under the herd law. Several juvenile fracases took place among Rees's brothers, Llewelyn's boys, and the Taylor sons.

Early in 1884, a new player entered the game when the Edwin Roberts family migrated from Wales to settle on land bordering Spring Ranch and the eighty-five acres James Taylor had plowed in 1881. Since his funds were limited and he wanted to increase his crop yield, Roberts inquired about renting some land.

Elizabeth Taylor rented an acreage to Roberts which had been used for pasture since 1881. One can only speculate about her motives at this time. Perhaps the fact that Roberts was also Welsh and could speak the language attracted her. For whatever reason, her frequent visits to the Roberts home set tongues wagging. There was no love lost between Elizabeth and Roberts' wife, yet she let him have a wagon team and some hogs on credit until harvest, without the formality of a promissory note.

During the summer of 1884, Elizabeth Taylor spent much time commuting to surrounding towns making livestock deals. Her sons stayed at the sod house but were more than a bit mischievous. Rees T. Rees's crippled brother Isaac became an object of their taunts and jibes when they spotted him in Rees's fields.

Before summer's end, Elizabeth was besieged with complaints about her livestock downing fences and trampling fields. Because of the increased problems, she hired a full-time hand to ride fence and watch her stock. The new hand's surveillance lessened the complaints for a time until he discovered John Llewelyn's boys pulling down one of their own father's pasture fences. After warning the boys, the hand reported the incident to Elizabeth.

When Llewelyn stormed up the hill to her house demanding reparations, Elizabeth curtly informed him she would pay no claim because she had a witness to the so-called fence pulling. When the ranch hand gave his version of the episode, Llewelyn was furious. He refused to believe his obedient sons would do such a thing. Because she had a witness and felt comfortable that, if the matter came to court, she would be exonerated, Elizabeth told him to go ahead and file a complaint. Llewelyn stomped out of her house ranting that he would do just that, after he made a few uncomplimentary remarks about Elizabeth which her sons heard.

Next was the matter of a choice timber stake on the Blue River that Elizabeth claimed which was cause for dispute and litigation. Claimants stated Elizabeth was using the tract only for grazing, even though she planted a good stand of trees on the land. Now they wanted access to that timber.

While the timber question simmered, on October 4, Llewelyn, Rees, and Beyer delivered William and John Taylor, bound and trussed, to their mother. This time, Llewelyn informed the woman her sons had been caught pulling down his fence. He had two witnesses and was on his way to swear out a complaint.

After the men left, she questioned the boys, who readily admitted their guilt. They said they were merely getting even with Llewelyn for the things he had said about her.

On October 23, after John Llewelyn testified, District Attorney G.W. Benius handed down an indictment stating William and John Taylor "did wantonly and maliciously lay down, prostrate, deface and injure a fence enclosing pasture land of John Llewelyn." Bail was set at $200. Elizabeth secured $150 of this amount from L.A. Payne, the banker in the nearby town of Harvard, by

Standing on a load of logs which now filled their own wagon, Roberts and Beyer came slowly toward the boys. William and John urged their horses faster and started to yell insults. The noise broke the silence of the winter afternoon and caused the Roberts team to shy. (Illustrations by Mick Harrison)

giving him a quit claim deed to one of her quarter sections. The boys were released into her custody and the case was scheduled for trial during the May, 1885, term of District Court at Clay Center.

During the last two weeks of January 1885, Beyer, Roberts, and others helped themselves to trees on the disputed timber claim. Beyer and Roberts, in particular, turned deaf ears to Elizabeth's complaints over the matter. Legally, she had no recourse until the matter was settled in court. On January 8, when she saw them going past her house toward the timber, she warned them not to cut down any more trees. None of the men on the wagon paid any attention to her angry shouts. Roberts merely whipped the horses faster. She was left fuming over what to do next.

Later that afternoon, some distance from their own land, William and John Taylor were riding in a wagon when Roberts and Beyer came into sight. Standing on a load of logs which now filled their own wagon, Roberts and Beyer came slowly toward the boys. William and John urged their horses faster and started to yell insults. The noise broke the silence of the winter afternoon and caused the Roberts team to shy. Beyer fell from the logs to the road. Although he was badly stunned, Beyer heard a shot fired as the Taylor wagon passed Roberts.

The Taylor boys then made a quick detour through open fields. Isaac Rees, out in one of his brother's fields, saw their wagon rushing by. He noticed William Taylor holding his mother's shotgun and wondered about it at the time.

Meanwhile, Rees T. Rees and several other men in front of Rees's house saw the Roberts wagon coming along, apparently without a driver. They rushed to the road and discovered Roberts lying on the logs with part of his face blown off. Then Joseph Beyer came running down the road, and when he saw Roberts' body, he swore the Taylor boys were responsible.

The five men carried Roberts' body to his sod house, where the wails of his wife and five children undoubtedly hastened their decision to go after the Taylor boys.

By mid-evening, William and John Taylor were in a Clay County jail cell. Elizabeth had followed the irate Rees and the others to the county seat, where she tried in vain to arrange bail. She engaged attorneys John Reagan and C.J. Dilworth, both of whom later became prominent in Nebraska legal and political circles, to defend her sons.

While the boys waited in jail, events rushed forward. One night in early March, some seventy-five horsemen gathered, took oaths of secrecy, and headed toward Elizabeth Taylor's house on the hill. There they shouted to the woman and her brother to come out, but their warnings were answered by gunfire. Facing a stubborn woman and her gun, the majority decided against taking the initiative and rode off. That left only the ringleaders of the group to dodge the repeated bursts of gunfire which continued for some time. Finally they retreated and went their separate ways — for that night at least. The next day, Elizabeth and Thomas moved down to the sod house on the Blue River. Its thick, earthen walls offered more security from marauders than did her wooden frame house.

Between March 8 and 13, John Llewelyn's barn mysteriously burned down. At Rees's urging, another vigilante meeting was arranged for on the night of March 14.

Perhaps their second attempt might have been unsuccessful had Elizabeth Taylor decided not to go to Hastings that morning, or had Thomas Jones and the other men in the house not relaxed their vigilance. When Elizabeth returned that fateful evening, she learned someone had entered her home and removed all their firearms and ammunition. Thus, when the mob came, the occupants could do nothing but surrender. Then, at last, Rees could stand on the iron and wooden bridge of the Blue River and watch the woman who had spurned him plead for her life.

When the Taylor boys' case came to trial in 1886, the defense pressed for dismissal, and they were judged

21

"not guilty" because the indictment for murder was "undecided."

The men who lynched Elizabeth Taylor and her brother were never charged or brought to trial. Although they were well known, no one in Clay County dared accuse them publicly.

Today, the somewhat battered, though impressive, marble shafts over Elizabeth's and Thomas' graves, and the solid stone marker above Edwin Roberts' grave some one hundred yards south and a few feet west of the Taylor plot, show no evidence of the violence they suffered.

Even a fragment of one of the mule halters used for the hangings seemed to have little effect on its owner. Mr. N.K. Newcomb of Clay Center, Nebraska, received a letter written June 8, 1913.

Dear Sir,

Enclosed is the relic we were talking about it is no good to me and may change my luck if I part with it. If to part with it we read in the good book that the Philistines sent the Ark back after a sort of no-good journey so as to have salved the conscience but this is not the case here.

Still feel sorry for Tom but his old gal got what she deserved.

He hopes all good things come to him who waits you never thought that you would be in possession of this rope. [sic]

Yours truly,
J.T. Anthes

For many years since, the frazzled, yellow fragment of rope, the letter, and the box the relic was delivered in have been in a small safe in the Clay County Clerk's office and may be reviewed upon request.

The Only Legal Hanging In Custer County

Men and women standing in the tightly-packed crowd craned their necks in the hope of catching a glimpse of the condemned man as he shuffled toward the scaffold. Dressed in a boiled white shirt, dark blue suit, and laced black shoes, the prisoner walked slowly between Sheriff W. Wood and Deputy G.B. Wood, his shoulders bowed in anticipation of the fate awaiting him.

Stumbling slightly as he began to climb the thirteen steps leading up to the scaffold platform eighteen feet above the ground, the man's eyes narrowed as he saw the hangman's rope dangling above a wooden chair placed over the trapdoor.

Johnny Lehman, of German ancestry, was born in Atlanta, Georgia, in 1839 or 1840. Upon reaching adulthood, he left home and lived in Wisconsin, Montana, and Nebraska, before arriving in Custer County, South Dakota, in the late 1880s.

He had been ranching for several years down on the lower French Creek, outside Custer, when he became embroiled in an argument with his neighbor, An-

24

thony Furman. It seems that Furman had fenced off some of Lehman's land. Incensed, Lehman publicly threatened Furman's life.

Custer County Deputy Sheriff John Burns arrested Lehman; the charge was assault with the intent to kill. Lehman quickly made bail and, as he left Custer City, commented he would "kill anyone sent to his ranch." While Lehman returned to his ranch, Judge George O. Sanderson discovered the bond amount to be insufficient, so he decided to send Sheriff Burns out to Lehman's ranch with a new arrest warrant.

Armed with the warrant, Sheriff Burns, accompanied by John Siebert, rented a team and wagon and left Custer City in the early afternoon of July 11, 1889. Burns had been to the Lehman ranch earlier and knew it was located by Fairburn, a small community close to Custer City.

When Burns and Siebert drove into the yard in front of Lehman's house, Lehman stepped outside holding a Spencer carbine in the crook of his arm; he was visibly agitated. Upon seeing this, Burns decided to leave. Siebert began to turn the wagon around, and Burns, who was watching Lehman closely, saw the angry rancher raise the Spencer to his shoulder. Burns yelled out, "Don't shoot, John, we are leaving!"

Lehman pulled the trigger, but the first cartridge was defective. Quickly chambering another cartridge into the gun, Lehman fired. The report of the Spencer rang across the valley, and Burns stiffened as the heavy slug ripped into his right side. As Burns fell back into the wagon, Siebert whipped the horses and raced off to safety.

25

Sheriff Burns died several hours later, never regaining consciousness. The following day a posse was formed in Custer City and went to Lehman's ranch, only to find he had taken off for parts unknown. Governor Arthur C. Mellette posted a $500 reward for the murderer, and before long, several posses were scouring the countryside.

Meanwhile, Lehman was reputed to have traveled through the Fall River country in Nebraska, and was even reported to have joined and ridden in one of the posses looking for him. His luck ran out on September 8, 1889, when the Fall River County sheriff arrested him near Rushville, Nebraska. He was found working on a farm under the name Benjamin Lawrence and did not resist arrest.

After being returned to Custer City, a series of events began that would include several trials and three death sentences, resulting in confusion and exasperation for the people of Custer City, South Dakota.

In December 1889, a grand jury indicted Lehman for murder. He was tried, convicted, and sentenced to hang. However, Judge John W. Nowlin did not believe he had been properly defended by Attorney W. H. Frye, so he set aside the verdict of the jury on September 4, 1890. A new trial began, with Frye and Charles J. Buell defending Lehman, while Edmund Smith and H.D. Reynolds prosecuted the case.

Again, Lehman was found guilty and was sentenced to hang on November 13, 1890. The day of his execution came and passed. The case was taken to the State Supreme Court, and in April 1891, the Court upheld the original verdict.

On September 21, 1891, Judge C.M. Thomas sentenced Lehman to hang on November 4, 1891. Lehman's attorneys petitioned Governor Mellette for clemency, but the request was denied, and Lehman's date with the hangman stood firm. The only problem was that a bill abolishing capital punishment had been passed in the state legislature at the same time, further complicating the case.

Citizens of Custer City believed that Lehman had been given all the fair trials he deserved and looked forward to his execution. All was going according to plan until Governor Mellette changed his mind on the morning of the execution and granted Lehman a stay. He felt that Lehman should have the opportunity to go before the State Board of Pardons and have his case reviewed.

The reaction to this was one of "manifest disgust," according to the *Custer Chronicle*, which also reported occasional threats of lynching. Because the citizens had gone to great expense erecting a scaffold and inviting guests to the event, "they raised a merry howl."

In response to Lehman's going to the State Board of Pardons, the townspeople petitioned the Governor, asking that the original sentence be carried out. The request contained the signatures of the original twenty-four jurors from Lehman's earlier trial and three-quarters of the taxpayers of the county.

On December 3, 1891, C. L. Wood and C.J. Buell appeared before the Board and asked that Lehman be sentenced to life. The Board denied the request, because they felt that this was not the question in this case and thus should not be considered.

The hanging was rescheduled for January 5, 1892. Custer authorities rebuilt the scaffold and erected a high wooden fence around the courthouse yard, but, again, all their work went for naught. Governor Mellette offered Lehman a reprieve as a result of what one observer called, "a base use of the technicalities of the law." Using this delay to Lehman's advantage, lawyers won a retrial on the grounds that he was insane at the time of the earlier trials. This compelled one Custer editor to suggest that Lehman would "die all right, of senility."

This trial took place on January 7, 1892, before Judge Gardsy in Custer, and for the third time he was found guilty. The execution date was set for February 19, 1892.

Defense attorneys Wood and Buell applied to the State Supreme Court for a writ of Certiorari (a review of all previous proceedings), but it was refused. Governor Mellette was again ready to interfere, but this time he declined. The execution was reset for the same date.

While all this legal hassle was taking place, Lehman was being kept in a steel cell located in the Custer County Courthouse, on the west edge of Custer City. After Governor Mellette's second reprieve, Lehman was quoted as saying, "I knew this thing about hanging me was nonsense. They've been trying to hang me for two years and haven't got the job done yet. My lawyers are too good for them."

Of course, now that he was finally going to hang, Lehman's attitude wasn't as cocky. He watched as a local sawmill operator built a gallows and a fence twenty feet square and eight feet high behind the courthouse. The trap-door system was one that worked by a series of connecting rods featuring a level-like ratchet device. Invitations were sent out, and chairs were set up in the courtyard.

The night before the execution, Lehman slept relatively well. He awoke at seven a.m. and ate a good breakfast. Later in the morning, he became sullen and moody, making the comment, "Let them come, I am ready."

At eleven a.m., new clothes arrived for the condemned man, but the pants were too long, so he was given shorter ones which made him feel better. He ate lunch at noon and was visited by H.D. Reynolds and a Reverend Tracy. Lehman reportedly commented to Reynolds, "Had I been defended as well as I was prosecuted, I wouldn't be hung today."

He told the Reverend Tracy he was a Catholic, but when he was asked to confess and pray he replied, "Praying is not my business. That is your profession. You pray for me, and if I have done anything wrong, that will make it all right."

At 2:30 p.m., Sheriff Wood and Deputy G.B. Wood arrived and fastened Lehman's hands behind his back. As they walked him out to the gallows, Lehman knew the game was up.

As they sat him down in the chair over the trap-door, strapped him in, and tied his hands once again, Wood asked, "John, have you anything to say?"

"I want to say to the audience and spectators that you are cruel men and are murdering me."

Sheriff Wood then placed the black death hood over the trembling murderer's head and signaled the executioner to drop the trap-door. The body dropped and, after several minutes of twitching and convulsive jerks, was still. It had hung for twenty minutes when, at 3:15 p.m., it was removed and laid out in the courthouse for people to view. It was noted that in death his face still showed the brutality and ugliness that it had in life.

After a time, the body was taken to the basement where a post-mortem was performed by Dr. Taylor and Dr. Phipps. The brain was removed and dissected. Dr. Taylor believed Lehman to be sane and wanted to prove his trial comments regarding this allegation. To his satisfaction, the brain weighed 46 3/4 ounces, was proportionately developed, and seemed healthy.

To the satisfaction of the Custer townspeople, Johnny Lehman was finally laid to rest. Thus ended the only legal hanging recorded in Custer City, South Dakota.

Rope used to hang Johnny Lehman in February 1892. Lehman was accused of murdering Deputy Sheriff John Burns, tried three times, and found guilty three times even though his sanity continued to be in question. (John Heasley, Custer, SD)

The Committee of 33

By the mid-1880s, the town of Hastings, Nebraska, had become one of the fastest growing cities in the Midwest. Founded by a group of English immigrants in 1871 and named after Major Thomas Del Monte Hastings, a construction engineer for the Burlington Northern Railroad, the city was located on the St. Joseph-Denver Railroad line, sixteen miles south of the Platte River in the central part of the state.

Between 1871 and 1885, the population of Hastings had more than doubled. Permanent institutions such as banks, schools, and industries had been established. The rough, lumber shacks of the 1870s were replaced by solid, Victorian homes with stairs, verandas, and turrets. Residents of Hastings boasted that the newly built Kerr Opera House was the best of its kind between Denver and Omaha. It was a time of great change as the town grew and prospered.

The people in this growing, progressive town were shocked by sensational incidents that took place in the latter part of March 1883. That month would see the brutal murder of a prominent Hastings businessman and the vigilante-style lynching of two of his killers.

Cassius M. Millett was the proud owner of a dry goods store located in a red brick, two-story building on the main street of Hastings. The location was perfect for his store. It sat on the north side of Second Street, halfway between busy Hastings and Denver avenues. Millet had worked hard to build up his business and had established himself as an honest, reputable businessman.

Throughout the cold, late winter afternoon of March 26, 1883, Millet had observed three strangers walking suspiciously up and down the rough wooden plank sidewalk in front of his store. Normally, that would not have concerned the merchant, but the mens' appearance, as well as their persistent interest in his store, struck him as more than a little odd. Two of the men were older than the third, and from their dirty, ragged looks Millet guessed they were vagrants. The third man, who was really no more than a boy, hesitantly seemed to follow the other two men.

Several times Millett caught the two older men staring in the large front window, but when he attempted to go outside and ask them what they wanted, they would quickly leave. The afternoon passed rapidly, as Millett busily worked throughout the store. That evening, after pulling the shades and locking the front door, he glanced up and down Second Street, wondering if he would see the three strangers. Not seeing the men, Millett wrapped his woolen scarf tightly around his neck to protect him against the biting March wind and proceeded to walk the four blocks to his two-story home in the fashionable part of the city.

The next day seemed to go as usual for the hardworking Millett. Throughout the day he would glance up from stocking shelves and waiting on customers, but he did not notice the men from the previous day. After closing and locking the store for the evening, he once again started for home in the crisp, late afternoon, not suspecting the events that were about to take place.

As he walked down the red brick sidewalk, watching the winter sun set on the horizon of the western prairie, he felt the presence of someone following him. Turning quickly, Millett's knees weakened, and his heart jumped. He recognized the three men from the day before walking behind him. When not more than a quarter of a block away, the trio donned cloth masks and ran up to Millett, brandishing Colt revolvers. Their purpose, as later confessed in the court arraignment, was to take Millett to a cave west of town and rob him.

The robbers took their victim westward on foot with one of the men threatening to kill Millett if he cried out for help. As the group neared the black iron gate of Millett's neighbor, Aaron May, the terrified storekeeper decided to attempt an escape. Suddenly, Millet broke away from the masked men. Running through the gate, he tried to reach the four-foot fence separating his house from his neighbors. One of the older robbers, seeing Millett running frantically towards the fence, raised his revolver, took aim, and fired. The sharp report of the revolver echoed up and down the quiet neighborhood. Millett staggered as the bullet struck him squarely between the shoulder blades. With superhuman effort, he climbed the fence and stumbled across the yard to his back door. There he fell into the arms of his wife, lapsing into unconsciousness.

Regaining consciousness for a short time later that evening, Millett was able to give a statement to Isaac Le-Dioyt, a notary public, describing the vicious assault. Surrounded by his family, Millett died that night and was buried April 1 with all the laurels given to a veteran of the Grand Army of the Republic.

Meanwhile, the efficient Hastings Police Department, led by Police Chief J.C. Williams, was doing some fine detective work. Upon fleeing the scene of the crime, one of the highwaymen had carelessly dropped his mask on the sidewalk in front of Millett's house. The mask was found by the daughter of W.A. Hall, who quickly delivered it to Police Chief Williams. Williams knew immediately where the mask had come from since he had just investigated a report of a table cover stolen from the St. Louis Boarding House located on South Street. The material of the table cover and the mask matched perfectly. The table cover had been removed from a room that belonged to a man named James Green. Suspicion immediately fell on him and two known colleagues — Fred Ingraham, a man about Green's age, and John Babcock, who was only eighteen years old. Police Chief Williams knew the three were digging a well for a farmer named Charles Kohl. Assembling several deputies, they all rode to Kohl's farm a few miles south of Hastings and arrested all three men. None of the fugitives put up a fight when they were arrested.

Cassius Millett had been a popular businessman in Hastings, and as news of his murderers' arrest spread through the town, talk of lynching quickly grew. Attorney Charles H. Dietrich, also a prominent Hastings native, heard the talk while attending a dance that night at Liberal Hall. Not convinced they were guilty, he took it upon himself to launch his own murder investigation. After securing a permit from Mayor W.H. Lanning, he interviewed Babcock, the youngest of the three accused men. Dietrich was able to obtain a full confession from him. Alone and scared, Babcock convinced Dietrich that he had been drawn into the plot by the older Ingraham and Green. From that point on, Dietrich was determined to save the young man from being lynched.

It was a chilly, gray morning on April 3, 1883, when the three prisoners were brought to a building called the "Stone Block," a two-story, yellowish stone structure that was one of the newest building in downtown Hastings. Located on the corner of Second Street and Denver Avenue, it housed the County Courthouse and jail. Arraigned in front of Federal District Judge Work, Babcock was the only one of the three men who pleaded guilty to the murder charge. Attorney Dietrich and Babcock had decided that he should plead guilty, hoping his honesty and frank admission of guilt would work in his favor.

After the arraignment, the shackled prisoners were placed under special protective custody in the small, cramped jury room just off the courtroom. Mayor Lanning placed special deputies W. Cutter, J.E. Hutchinson, Edward Burton, and J.P. Farr in charge of the uneasy prisoners. Meanwhile, Dietrich, working tirelessly behind the scene, had managed to get William Lanning to name him as one of the special deputies guarding the men. He knew trouble was brewing and wanted to be near Babcock if it became a reality.

Later that evening, a meeting was held under the light of flickering torches in a lumberyard south of the Burlington Northern railroad tracks. The torchlight threw dark shadows across the masked faces of thirty-three men gathered there. One man stood on a large stack of lumber and assigned numbers to the rest. When he finished, a roll call was taken. Given their mood, it was evident that if the vigilantes had their way, the three prisoners would never go to trial. Picking up a large wooden timber that could be used as a battering ram, the thirty-three men started toward the Stone Block several blocks away.

Back at the Stone Block, the prisoners were restless. Knowing their lives were in danger, they kept asking the deputies if they had heard anything about any lynching plans. They were answered with grim silence. Around 10:00 p.m., the Committee of 33 arrived at the Stone Block. Yelling wildly, they ran up the wooden stairs to the second floor and slammed the battering ram against the heavy wooden door to the jury room. The door barely budged after the first blow. They struck it again, shattering it.

Rushing into the dimly lit room with pistols drawn, the Committee seized the prisoners. The vigilantes' grim determination convinced the frightened guards that resistance would be futile. Placing ropes around the necks of the terrified prisoners, the Committee dragged them from their beds, marched them downstairs and threw them into a waiting buggy.

About a mile north of the city stood a bridge on the St. Joseph-Grand Island Railroad. The Committee had predetermined that the railroad trestle would be a perfect spot for the lynching. When the group arrived, ropes were hurriedly tied to the tracks and around the necks of the doomed men. Unable to find a way to save Babcock, Dietrich, too, made his way to the lynching site. Unfortunately, until then, there hadn't been an opportunity that allowed him to try any type of rescue.

The three condemned men trembled and pleaded for their lives in the cold night air. Standing side by side upon the wooden railroad ties, they looked down on the masked faces of the crowd and realized their time on earth had come to an end. Suddenly, one member of the Committee stepped behind Green and Ingraham and shoved

Later to become governor of Nebraska, Charles H. Dietrich made a desperate attempt to save young John Babcock from the lynch mob. (Nebraska State Historical Society)

them off the bridge. As their weight pulled the ropes taut, the mens' faces contorted into masks of horrible agony. Seeing that the sobbing Babcock was next, Dietrich readied the sharp-edged hunting knife he had been concealing in his belt. When the men pushed Babcock from the railroad trestle, he cut the rope with the knife.

As Babcock fell to the frozen ground below the bridge, the vigilantes crowded angrily around Dietrich demanding an explanation. His voice ringing clear in the night air, Dietrich recited the story of Babcock's confession. Standing above the prostrate Babcock, Dietrich told the Committee that he had promised the young man a fair trial and declared for all to hear that he planned to make good his promise. After a short consultation, the Committee decided to take Babcock back to town, leaving Ingraham and Green to twist silently in the cold darkness of the April night.

The lifeless bodies of Ingraham and Green hung until ten o'clock the next morning. Official records note that trains stopped that morning to let passengers view the unfortunate men. An inquisition was held by Adams County Sheriff Hutchinson, whereupon a verdict of death by strangulation was officially entered. The bodies were cut down and buried in Potter's Field, a cemetery for the poor and vagrant, located in northwest Hastings.

John Babcock, the young man who was saved from the lynching that night, was tried in Adams County

Scene of the lynching of Fred Ingram and Jas. Green, murderers of C.M. Millet by the bold "33" on Tuesday night, April 3rd, 1883, at Hastings, Nebraska. (Geo. O. Churchill, Hastings, NE, Adams County Historical Society)

Court. He was sentenced to ten years at the state penitentiary in Lincoln, Nebraska. There he learned the art of stone cutting. Released after seven years, Babcock disappeared and was never heard from again.

Charles H. Dietrich, the brave man who risked his own life that night in order to see justice done, went on to an illustrious career as a United States Senator and, eventually, as Governor of Nebraska.

For months after the lynching, few Hastings residents talked about the Committee of 33 and the events that took place that night in April. No one ventured any harsh criticism, fearing that a member of the vigilantes might be listening. The vigilantes were a secret organization, and their membership was never made public. They were, nonetheless, a potent force in maintaining law and order in Hastings' early years.

In July 1883, ghostly visitants were observed by Hastings residents at the St. Joseph-Grand Island Railroad bridge north of the city. Several people reported seeing two ghostly figures approach the bridge and appear to inspect it. Other people, also visiting the spot, reported the presence of an unapproachable ghostlike figure demonstrating an acute interest in the "hanging bridge."

The Lynching of Kid Wade

Boy Horsethief

On the morning of February 8, 1884, the small village of Bassett, in Rock County, Nebraska, awoke horrified to learn that it had been host to a lynching party during the night. The body of a young man named Kid Wade was found hanging from a railroad whistling post a mile east of town.

For a number of years, the Niobrara River country of northern Nebraska had been infested by gangs of horse thieves. One of the most active was headed by a character named Doc Middleton, who was captured after a colorful career and sentenced to prison in 1879.

Among the members of the Doc Middleton gang was a youngster named Albert Wade — better known to the locals as Kid Wade. Wade was described as being about nineteen or twenty years of age, about five foot seven or eight inches tall and weighing around one-hundred-forty pounds. He reportedly dressed in the usual frontier costume of boys and young men at the time — buckskin shirt, large neck handkerchief, chaps, white cowboy hat, boots, spurs, and a gun belt. Wade frequently traveled with a friend who became known as

"White Stockings," but whose real name was never discovered.

Although not a true "bad man," he was generally known as a horse thief and, if cornered, could be dangerous. When Doc Middleton was arrested, Wade escaped amidst a hail of bullets. He then headed for safer country to pursue his occupation. A year later, the Kid was arrested on a farm two miles west of Sioux City, Iowa. Although it was generally believed that he was a member of the Middleton gang, the only formal charge brought against him was that of stealing a pony. He was tried, convicted, and sentenced to three years in prison.

Albert "Kid" Wade entered prison on November 25, 1879, and after an uneventful stay, was released on June 7, 1882. The time spent at the Iowa Anamosa State Penitentiary evidently had little reformative influence on the Kid. In late 1883 he resumed horse stealing operations along the Niobrara near Carns, Nebraska, where twenty-five to thirty horses were stolen. Among the horses taken (near Morris Bridge on the Niobrara River) were six owned by a Henry Richardson and two from a Reverend Clifton

This sudden flurry of horse stealing caused quite a furor. Since Middleton's gang had been broken up several years earlier, the countryside had been fairly quiet. Now that the stealing had started up again, the local settlers were not about to stand for it. A new county had been formed, but permanent officers had not yet been appointed, so the settlers met and formed a secret vigilante committee named the Niobrara Mutual Protective Association, informally known as the "Regulators." It was primarily composed of settlers from the vicinity of Morris Bridge. The NMPA was a secret organization with a con-

Kid Wade (National Archives)

stitution and by-laws drawn up by attorney A.J. "Cap" Burnham who was homesteading in the area. Eighteen men signed the document.

Several days later, a number of Kid's new gang, including Andy Culbertson and William Morris, were arrested at Kid Wade's camp in Middleton's Canyon on Holt Creek. Wade and another outlaw named Eph Weatherwax were able to escape. Culbertson soon "spilled" his .guts about their activities hoping for lenient treatment from the angry vigilantes.

Events moved rapidly. Henry Richardson, accompanied by three other men from "Cap" Burnham's "Regulators," set out for the Black Hills in search of the fugitive horsethieves and the stolen stock. On January 14, 1884, Richards wrote a letter about the trip...

"I write you that myself and party have returned from the west, and are pretty worn out with the trip. I found that Andy Culbertson told a very straight story. I found things just as he stated. I found every horse where he said it was. We found twenty one head of horses and brought sixteen head back with us. We had a hard, cold trip, but we are all ready and willing to do the same thing again should occasion require it. Now I think that

Doc Middleton during horse thief days. (Nebraska State Historical Society)

we have given the rustlers a good starter. We have left them a good pair to draw to, and I think that if the deck isn't kept well shuffled they will fill it by spring."

Meanwhile, Wade and his companions drove the stolen horses north to the Black Hills, then followed the White River to the Missouri, down to the mouth of the Niobrara where they started back west on the north side through Indian country.

Until now, Kid had kept all the stolen horses, but when he turned westward, he began selling them along the way. It was this practice that ultimately led to his capture. Among the stolen horses was one with a split hoof, a easily detected mark. He sold this horse to a farmer. Evidently he saw his blunder almost immediately and returned and bought the horse back. The farmer was naturally suspicious and followed Wade a short distance to see what would happen. Wade and a helper drove the horse out a mile or so, shot, and buried it. The farmer notified the local peace officers who dug it up and identified it as one of those stolen near Carns. From the description given to them, they recognized Kid Wade as one of the two men.

Wade was traced to Iowa where he was captured near LeMars, a couple of months later, having hidden in the Broken Kettle country near the Dakota line. They found him holed up in a house owned by a man named Mansfield. The house was built up on a dirt embankment and surrounded by a high wooden-board fence. The front door of the house was locked and the only other entrance was through a small door.

Because Wade was considered to be a desperate character, it was deemed wisest to resort to strategy in order to get him out of the house. Four of the men— Captain C.C. Dodge, Charles Messenger, Michael Coleman, and Peter Hanson, all of Greeley, Holt County— held a council and selected Messenger to approach the Mansfield farmhouse on the pretext of buying a horse. In order to divert suspicion, he bought a horse from a neighboring farmer. He then traveled to the Mansfield farm and bought a horse from Wade. He pretended that he did not have enough cash money with him and asked Wade to accompany him to Lemars where he would pay the balance in full. Wade readily agreed to accompany Messenger to LeMars where he thought he would receive the balance due him for the sale.

44

The two men set out on horseback with Messenger riding the horse he bought from Wade, and Wade riding Messenger's. They went to a livery barn in LeMars, dismounted and, in the next instant, Kid found himself covered by four Winchester rifles. He surrendered without a struggle and, according to the local paper, even turned over his saddle to Messenger as a gift.

Wade was taken from LeMars to Yankton, South Dakota. The YANKTON PRESS dated January 19, 1884, describes their arrival at the Commercial Hotel shortly before dark as, "rough looking men, four of them heavily armed and the fifth handcuffed." No reason was given for Wade being taken to Yankton, but it was stated that he had hired a team and wagon at the Steffins Livery Barn two months earlier and had not returned it to them.

He was taken to the O'Neill, Nebraska, area by the end of January where he was placed in custody. The January 24th O'Neill Frontier described the prisoner as a "decidedly unsophisticated youth of about twenty-three years of age who looked more like a farmhand than a thief," adding that those who knew of Kid's activities said that what he lacked in age, he more than made up in experience.

A dispatch from O'Neill on February 3rd, reported that Wade was in the custody of the Regulators near Red Bird and was telling all he knew. It had been agreed upon that he was guilty, but most people did not believe that he would "squeal." When Wade learned that others were placing the blame on him, he made up his mind to tell all and take his chances with the law.

From Red Bird, Wade was taken to the north side of the Niobrara River, then west toward Carns. He was in

Kid Wade's Last Journey. Route taken by vigilantes with Kid Wade as Prisoner from Red Bird to Whistling Post at Bassett, Nebraska, February 3-8, 1884. (Drawn by Miss T. Josephine Haugen)

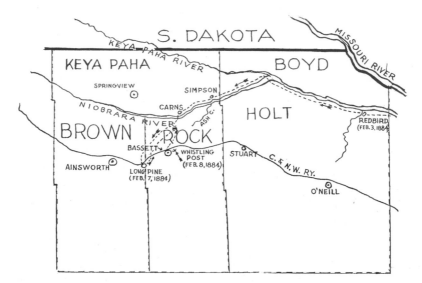

the custody of Richardson, Kinney, and Honnen when they stopped at the Haugen farm for lunch. The question was later asked whether the Kid displayed any apprehension about his possible fate. According to Mrs. Haugen, the prisoner showed no signs of concern or remorse. He played with a doorknob and laughed freely as he answered Richardson's questions. To one query about his whereabouts in the past, he gave the reply, "Yes, I've had many warm breakfasts at your house."

After lunch, the four traveled to Carns where they again crossed the Niobrara. That evening, three other men came to ask accommodations for the night. They, too, were seeking the Kid, but whether or not they belonged to the same vigilante company was not learned.

The February 2nd *O'Neill Frontier*, reported that an effort had been made to secure Wade by the Holt County authorities, but that Sheriff Hersheiser had missed connections and the Kid remained safely guarded in nearby Brown County. It also expressed satisfaction that Holt County would be spared the expense of prosecution and further expressed the hope that there might be "no delay nor foolishness" in dealing with the famous horse thief.

The *Long Pine Journal* of February 13, 1884, throws much light on the subsequent move of the Regulators.

On Tuesday afternoon our town was set agog when Kid Wade, the notorious horse thief who has operated so extensively in this part of the country the past several years and who was recently captured in Iowa, was brought in by one Kinney, a sort of lieutenant to Capt. Burnham. The Kid is a young man of less than 25 years, of rather slender build, a shambling gait, a low forehead and massive jaws, and a face inclined to angular and sharp features, on which the beard scarcely yet grows; in fact the general makeup of the man, and especially the facial expression is one more fitting a levee loafer or sneak thief than one denoting the higher aspirations of a horse thief. The object of the Vigilantes in bringing the prisoner before the public was to give the people an opportunity to question him as to his treatment since capture, and thus refute the charges that have been made against the Vigilantes as to their "holding up" their prisoners and extorting confessions from them at the rope's end, and other inhuman-like atrocities they have been accused of practicing in their pursuit of evidence against criminals.

The Kid said he had been well treated, his appearance voluntary, and any statements he made were wholly of his own free will; that he had not been intimidated by threats of violence, or influenced by promise of leniency — but it was the only means left him of retaliating upon numerous parties who had been 'rounded up' by Vigilantes, and who strove to throw all blame on him, suing for their mercy in dire necessity, and seeking vindication through his abundance of guilt. He denies any knowledge of a regularly organized band of thieves as has been so believed and reported; and his statements, if true, serious implicate several heretofore prominent citizens of this county as being in complicity with the thieves, and measures will soon be taken to establish their innocence or prove their guilt.

Tuesday night another party of Vigilantes, controlled by one Captain Burnham, arrived and relieved Kinney of the prisoner, saying they should take Wade to Holt County, where he would be held for trial, before the proper authorities, and on Wednesday forenoon left for Long Pine with their charge, going in a northerly direction from town.

He was then taken to Morris Bridge, fifteen miles northeast of Carns, and turned over to the sheriff of Holt County, Ed Hersheiser, who was waiting for him. They headed for Bassett, Nebraska, arriving about 7:30 p.m., and put up for the night in Martin's Hotel. Wade preferred lying on the floor on a blanket to going to bed, and was disposed in the same room where the sheriff and several other deputies kept a watchful vigil on the doomed boy.

About midnight, a band of a dozen masked men entered the room with revolvers drawn and ordered, "All hands up!" With hands raised, Wade was aroused and marched off. Knowing full well the penalty he might soon pay, he begged for their mercy, promising to lead a better life. He used all his powers of persuasion in an attempt to gain a respite from the fate quickly approaching. His appeals fell on deaf ears, and he was dragged away with the masked men forbidding anyone to follow under the threat of death. The next morning, Wade was found hanging from a railway whistling post on the outskirts of Bassett.

It's interesting to note the route that was followed by the Regulators in taking Wade on his last ride. The arrest was made for stealing horses in Brown County and the proper place for holding trial should have been Ainsworth, Nebraska, the Brown county seat. O'Neill is east and slightly south of Long Pine. There was no logical reason for the prisoner to be taken fifteen miles northeast and toward the canyons of the Niobrara. Further, had the Holt County authorities so desired, they could have easily obtained Wade while he was held by the Regulators near O'Neill.

It was held for years that the devious route taken from Red Bird in Holt County, following the Niobrara on the north side of Carns, southwest to Long Pine, then northeast again, and finally back to Bassett, was used to prevent Wade from getting a legal trial.

The *Omaha World-Herald* of February 9, 1884, listed an interview of interest regarding this matter. The names of those interviewed were not given.

"Wade was alive last Sunday, for I saw him and talked with him. That was at the house of Dr. Richardson in Brown County. The doctor is, after Captain Burnham, the leader of the Regulators. Kid was brought in Saturday night and we asked to see him. Richardson told the men in the room, about twenty five, that he wanted the room. Next Wade was brought in. He had foot irons on. My friend asked him about some stolen stock. Kid answered to the point, telling who stole the stock and where it was when he last heard. My friend asked if Kid told the truth; that Kid was willing to give away the horse thieves who had peached on him, but not willing to give up points about men he considered to be his friends. Richardson went on to say they proposed to get the whole truth if they had to choke it out with a rope. Wade was taken away that night. He had been promised that he would be turned over to the civil authorities for trial, as other members of his gang had been."

No matter what happened and why, Bassett residents had no inkling of what occurred until the body was discovered hanging from the post the next morning. Wade was cut down and brought to a store in Ainsworth, Nebraska, and laid on the counter where Coroner Shafford made his examination. After a quick look, Shafford informed the public that Wade had died by hanging at the hands of "parties unknown." His hands were tied together, and a common halter rope was around his broken neck. The corpse was frozen stiff. After the brief inquest, he was laid on a pile of cordwood in front of the store.

When the west bound train arrived the next morning, the passengers saw the dead horse thief, and all wanted a piece of the rope he was hung with as a souvenir. The rope was cut into small pieces and given away. The next day, Wade was buried on top of Bassett Hill.

A side note to this story concerns Wade's father, a man of about fifty. He came to Carns and made inquiries about his dead son. He talked about prosecuting the vigilantes, and made statements that he would spend whatever amount of money it took to find the guilty parties. He left Carns and was later found partly buried with his feet sticking out of the ground. The body was said to have been mutilated and the fingernails cut off.

For years after this incident, rumor had it that Kid Wade had already decided to quit horse stealing and was going to publicly expose members of his gang. It was said that more than one member of the "Regulators" were afraid if he squealed they might have been incriminated, thus accounting for his "necktie party" on that winter night.

Why, if the law-abiding citizens felt the law should have been permitted to take its course, was no investigation made into the lynching of Kid and the murder of his father? Possibly, there were two reasons. First, the Wade family had a bad reputation and probably many thought they got what was coming to them anyway. Secondly, it appears none of the decent settlers wanted to get involved, a reason familiar even today. The country was sparsely settled at this time and "decent" people were thankful for being permitted to go about their lives hoping that, if they strictly attended to their own affairs, they would not be molested. Why take a chance and get into trouble themselves?

Time usually adds its legendary note to the details of pioneer tragedies, and the fate of Kid Wade is no exception. Perhaps the most fantastic tale was that the body was exhumed and the bones used at initiations in one of the Bassett lodges.

The Great Pawnee Massacre

nited States Superintendent of Indian Affairs Barclay White smiled as the steady stream of Pawnee men, women, and children rode their ponies past his front porch. They were on their way to the buffalo-rich Republican River Valley many miles to the southwest. It was the summer of 1873, and the Republican band of the Pawnees were happy to be leaving their reservation near Genoa, Nebraska, in search of the buffalo that still roamed the southwestern part of Nebraska.

The young men of the tribe were bored and looking forward to the semi-annual hunt with great anticipation. Little did they know that they were headed for a tragic confrontation with their mortal enemies, the Sioux.

Barclay White had selected John W. Williamson to be the trail agent to accompany the Pawnee. It was customary for agents to go with the Indians on their hunts to protect them from white men or hostile tribes. Williamson, a white employee of the Pawnee Agency, was popular among the Pawnee. They had given him two names, Bukskariwi (Curly Hair) and Chaikstaka Laket (White Man Leader).

A young college student named L.B. Platt was also on the hunt that summer. He had been staying at his uncle's house near the reservation during the vacation months and asked permission to join the Pawnee. Since he had been brought up close to the Indians and knew their ways, he was allowed to go.

Sky Chief was selected by the Pawnee to lead the hunt. As head chief of the Kit-ka-haws, or Republican band of the Pawnee, he was known as a great chief, honest, brave, and true to his friends. Other Indian leaders who went on the hunt were Fighting Bear (Koruska tapuk) and Sun Chief (Sakuru lasher). Sun Chief was the nephew of the great head chief, Pitalesharo.

As they left the agency in late June 1873, Williamson counted 250 men, 100 women, and 50 children, all mounted on horseback with 100 extra ponies to carry the anticipated packs of dried buffalo meat and hides. Superintendent White had given specific instructions to hunt the Republican River Valley but not to travel north of the Republican River into Sioux territory.

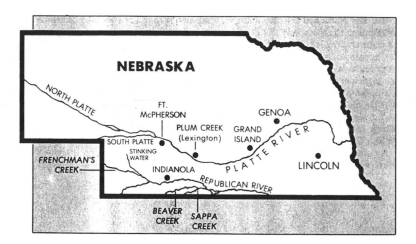

By July, the Pawnee hunting party was beyond the reservation. They followed the shallow Platte River until reaching what is now Grand Island, Nebraska. From there they turned south, reaching the Republican River, where they found and killed fifty-five buffaloes. Sky Chief was happy that they had found buffalo so quickly, and was anxious to reach his favorite hunting spot, Beaver Creek. Arriving there, the Pawnees killed another 400 buffalo, preparing the meat and hides as they went.

Continuing to follow Beaver Creek to the west, they encountered several white hunters who warned them of a large group of Sioux near by. The Pawnee wisely turned southwest to avoid the Sioux and hunted along Sappa Creek, but were unable to find any buffalo. Sky Chief held a council and decided the white hunters had invented the story about the Sioux in order to have the good hunting grounds to themselves.

The council's conclusion proved terribly wrong. Two large bands of Sioux warriors had come to the Republican River Valley from their agencies in northwest Nebraska, supposedly to hunt buffalo. Led by two white trail agents, Antoine Janis with the Oglala band, and Stephen Estes with the Sichangu Brulé band, the Sioux were supposed to stay north of the Republican River to hunt the northern buffalo herd. The Pawnee had many women and children with them to help with the hunt, but the two Sioux bands did not. It seemed unlikely the Sioux actually intended to hunt buffalo.

At the same time the Pawnee were hunting along Sappa Creek, the Oglalas set up camp on nearby Frenchman's Creek. Led by a chief called Little Wound, they were one day's ride from the band of Sichangus camping on the Stinking Water Creek. Both camps of Sioux warriors happened to be very near to the Pawnee.

Little Wound had been sending out scouts throughout July looking for the Pawnee. Finally, on August 1st, they found them. Although Little Wound knew he was not supposed to cross the Republican River to the south, he asked Trail Agent Janis if he had orders against their attacking the Pawnee hunting party. Unbelievably, Janis said no. He further indicated that although the Sioux could not fight their hereditary enemies in the vicinity of the Pawnee reservation, they certainly were not restricted from attacking them in the Republican River country.

Neither Janis or Estes attempted to stop the Sioux as they armed themselves and donned their fighting finery. Preventing over six hundred excited warriors from fighting would probably have been impossible anyway. The final act of this tragedy began.

Making a fateful decision, Sky Chief and his band of Pawnee turned north and started hunting along Driftwood Creek, killing almost two hundred buffalo. They moved farther and farther north, until another group of white hunters again warned them of a large number of Sioux nearby.

Another council was held. Agent Williamson urged the Pawnee to retire down the Republican to a grove of timber where they could organize a defensive position. Fighting Bear objected violently, saying that no sign of the Sioux had been found. He said again the white hunters made up the Sioux story in order to keep the best hunting for themselves. So that even if there were Sioux in the area, the Pawnee had whipped them before and could do so again. Although Williamson replied that they had come to hunt buffalo and not to fight the Sioux, he was overruled and the Pawnee began to break camp.

Sky Chief's decision not to follow the safe trail homeward along the south bank of the Republican sowed the seeds for his people's destruction. The Pawnee crossed the Republican and headed north, emerging on the plains near Frenchman's Fork. There they found large numbers of buffalo feeding on the open prairie. The men killed a large number of the shaggy beasts and, with the women's help, they were soon skinning them out.

The heat shimmered off the sun-baked prairie as Sky Chief worked skinning the large buffalo laying at his feet. Making an incision the length of the buffalo's belly with his keen-edged hunting knife, he became lost in his work. Suddenly, without warning, over three hundred Sioux thundered down from the surrounding hills. At the last moment, Sky Chief looked up and saw the Sioux warriors urging their ponies straight toward him. Grabbing his bow and quiver full of arrows, Sky Chief ran for his pony. As he mounted the frightened animal, several iron-tipped arrows struck him in the chest and he fell to the ground. The Sioux were upon him instantly, scalping the dead body. After killing several other hunters, the Sioux rode on toward the main Pawnee camp. Hearing Sioux war cries, the fear-stricken Pawnee men, women, and children rushed to the shelter of a nearby ravine. Agent Williamson rode out to parley with the Sioux, but a bullet whizzing past his ear cut short his attempt, forcing him to ride back to the relative safety of the canyon.

After several confused moments of trying to get the women and children on the pack horses, the remaining Pawnee hunters decided their best chance would be to confront their attackers. The outnumbered Pawnee rode out of the ravine and fought the Sioux. They held their own for about thirty minutes, until another group of three hundred Oglala Sichangus rode into view, attacking the beleaguered Pawnee from three sides.

The Pawnee turned and rode hard for safety, but by then the ravine had turned into a death trap. While the Pawnee men tried desperately to cut the buffalo hides and meat from the pack horses, the Sioux ringed the edge of the ravine and poured an intense fire directly down upon their hapless foes.

Before the Pawnee could escape the ravine, thirty-nine women, ten children, and several of the men were cut down. The Platt boy was captured by a Sioux warrior who took his firearms and ordered in a loud, firm voice, "You go!" The warrior pointed toward the Republican River. Platt ran away in terror, unaware the Sioux had strict orders from Estes and Janis not to harm any white men.

Those Pawnee who remained, fled the ravine in panic and streamed onto the flat prairie grassland. The Sioux pursued them for over three miles, killing more as they ran. Just when it seemed there would be no survivors, troops of the US 3rd Cavalry from Fort McPherson, under the command of a Major Russell, appeared from the cottonwoods lining the north side of the Republican River.

As soon as the Sioux saw the troopers deploying into battle formation, they murdered the Pawnee captives, sparing seventeen children, whom they carried off.

Major Russell had been warned by a man who reported to Fort McPherson about the potential conflict from a war party of Sioux that was loose and looking for trouble. When further word came that a Sioux war party was south of the river, troops were sent to the Republican in the hope of preventing a fight when and if the Pawnee and Sioux found each other. For all their efforts, the cavalry arrived an hour too late to prevent the slaughter.

The remaining Pawnee fled to the south side of the river. When an army officer called to them to come back across, none of the terrified Pawnee would recross the river. The officer, himself, finally had to cross to find out what had happened. Shortly, the cavalry gathered the remaining Pawnee and moved them down the south side of the river. Wailing and mourning, the Pawnee made camp near the site of present-day Indianola, Nebraska.

The tranquillity of Massacre Canyon belies its sanguinary name. This view is looking up the canyon from the southeast.
(Nebraska State Historical Society)

The Sioux attack was a complete success. They had carried off eighteen women and children, one hundred horses, the dried meat and hides of over eight hundred buffalo, and all the Pawnee firearms. They also took saddles, equipment, and anything else they could carry away.

The soldiers made notes of what happened and left the stiffening bodies of the dead Pawnee for the timber wolves. Williamson took the wounded on horses and pole drags to Plum Creek (now Lexington, Nebraska), where their wounds were dressed by a local doctor. The survivors made their way to Elm Creek, and then were transported by rail to Silver Creek, the station nearest to the reservation. Upon their arrival, Superintendent White concluded that 39 women, 10 children, and 20 men had been killed.

White sent a burial party to the Republican and also took testimony from the survivors. He valued the property lost at $3,000 and submitted a request to Congress that the sum be deducted from the money allocated to the Sioux. The money was sent as requested to the surviving Pawnee.

Congress also restricted the Sioux in their hunting across western Nebraska. In 1874, however, they were allowed to hunt wherever they pleased and were regularly supplied with food from a depot in Julesburg, Colorado.

While the Sioux went on to their great victory over Custer two years later, and eventually to defeat at Wounded Knee Creek in 1891, the murders at Massacre Canyon broke the back of the Pawnee tribe. In addition, because of the constant raiding and killing perpetrated by small bands of Sioux, the Pawnee concluded it would be wise to leave Nebraska and settle in what is now Oklahoma.

Traveling Bear, a great Pawnee warrior who had been cited for bravery and gallant conduct at the Battle of Summit Springs, July 11, 1869, lost his wife and all four of his children at Massacre Canyon. He, himself, was left for dead. Recovering consciousness at dark, he saw a Sioux warrior scalping a Pawnee body nearby. The Sioux walked over and stooped to scalp him, but Traveling Bear threw his arm around his enemy's neck, pulled him down, wrested the knife from him, and killed

Massacre Canyon Monument at dedication August 1930. Upper row: A.L. Taylor, Trenton; R.P. Colling, Clay Center; Ex-Governor Shallenberger, Alma; Rev. E.C. Grice, Trenton; and W.D. Otes, Trenton. Lower row: unidentified; Mrs. Anderson, Genoa, daughter of G.W. Williamson; J.W. Peretzel, Trenton; Mrs. Peterson, Genoa; and Mrs. Addison E. Sheldon, Lincoln.
(Nebraska State Historical Society)

him. Though seriously wounded, Traveling Bear made his escape, traveling 150 miles across country until he finally reached the Pawnee reservation. Unfortunately, he died a few months later, bringing the tragedy at Massacre Canyon to its final conclusion.

The Ash Hollow Massacre

and "Squaw Killer" William S. Harney

The Battle of Ash Hollow, fought in northwestern Nebraska on September 3, 1855, was the culmination of Brevet Brigadier General William S. Harney's Sioux Expedition. Harney's campaign marked the first time the United States Army had attempted a major expedition on the northern plains. It brought peace to the region that lasted until the Sioux uprising of 1862.

Though the battle is named for Ash Hollow, it actually took place more than six miles to the northwest on the opposite side of the North Platte River. Ash Hollow begins about four miles south of the North Platte. Its main canyon is formed by the confluence of several branches which drop abruptly from the table-land, forming a broad, flat ravine which runs almost north and debouches into the river valley. The battle received its name from a famous point on the California and Oregon Road, Ash Hollow, the nearest battlefield that had any name at all.

Harney's expedition was in retaliation for the Grattan "Massacre" (when Sioux Indians wiped out a thirty-man army detachment under Lieutenant John L. Gratton which was sent to punish the Sioux for killing an emigrant's cow) and other depredations attributed to the Brulé Sioux the previous year. Newspaper editors and Indian agents called for action after the Sioux attacked the Overland mail route between Fort Laramie and the South Fork of the Platte River. The army ordered Harney to mount a spring offensive.

Harney, born August 27, 1800, in Haysboro, Tennessee, received his commission as second lieutenant in the First Infantry in 1818. While stationed at Fort Warren, near Boston, Harney demonstrated a tendency to get into trouble when, in the absence of his commanding officer, he assumed command of the post. His commander ordered Harney court-martialled for his action. Although he was acquitted, it was the first of several such incidents. Harney was prone to speak out, take action, and worry about the results later. Such was the man in charge of chastising the Sioux.

While studying the upcoming campaign, Harney estimated that he could face up to 7,000 Indians ranging over a 90,000-square mile area. His orders were to prevent the Indians' escape and engage them in decisive battle. He had no idea what Sioux bands were responsible for the depredation and didn't think it was necessary to find out.

At Harney's disposal were one light battery of the 4th Artillery, four companies of the 2nd Dragoons, six companies of the 2nd Infantry, and six companies of the 6th Infantry. The force was the largest yet assembled in Nebraska Territory and included about 1,200 soldiers, or almost ten percent of the entire United States Army.

Harney planned to send a column of infantry, supported by a small mounted force, from some point on

*Harney and five companies under the command of Major
Albermarle Cady crossed the river and proceeded toward the
Indian village "with a view to attacking openly in concert with the
cavalry." Not until after the fight did Harney learn that trader Jim
Bordeaux sent a Brulé called Goose to warn of the soldiers'
approach.* (Ash Hollow Museum)

the North Platte River between Ash Hollow and Fort
Laramie to join another column of infantry. This column
was coming from Fort Pierre (in what is now South Dakota), north of the White River. Together they would
move toward the South Fork of the Cheyenne River and
then toward the Black Hills. The main body of cavalry,

with three companies of infantry from Fort Laramie, would be directed to penetrate the Black Hills in the direction of the North Fork of the Cheyenne. Harney hoped these movements would force the Indians to either give battle or desert their families just at the start of winter.

On April 1, 1855, Harney arrived at Jefferson Barracks in St. Louis, but preparations took three months, eliminating any chance of a spring offensive. At Fort Leavenworth in July, an angry Harney got off a few barbs to army headquarters in New York regarding the Indian Bureau and its management. He had had difficulty finding Indian guides, as they were afraid they would lose their annuities as well as wear out their good ponies chasing hostiles across the prairie. Harney singled out Commissioner of Indian Affairs George Manypenny, saying he had obstructed the campaign with "officious and pertinacious meddling." Harney also criticized the continued practice of traders giving arms to the Indians, and suggested the army should control such activity.

It was true the Indian Bureau had concerns about Harney's expedition. It feared the campaign would lead to "inflicting chastisement indiscriminately" and that innocent Indians would suffer as well as hostiles. The bureau had good reason to worry, as Harney had advised the adjutant general that he would not "hesitate to attack any body of 'hostile' Indians." It was common knowledge that Harney had said, "savages must be crushed before they are completely conquered," and that the way to "deal with the Indian is by first soundly whipping them before consenting to any peace talk." He was also quoted as having said to Edwin Morin, a French-Canadian trapper, "By God, I'm for battle—not peace."

At that same time, Thomas S. Twiss was named Upper Platte Indian agent and arrived at Fort Laramie on August 10, 1855. He sent runners to Indian camps with a notice that all friendly bands were to move south of the North Platte River. Those remaining in the north would be considered hostile and fair game for Harney's soldiers.

Most of the Indians moved south, but Little Thunder and others of the Southern Brulé (the Waz-za-za, Orphans, and Corn bands) remained north of the river. They had been hunting buffalo, gathering the meat they would need for the summer and fall, which to them had more priority than Twiss's order. As late as August 20, Twiss reported to Harney he did not know the precise locations of the hostile bands, but he expected to receive word soon.

By that time, Harney's forces had reached Fort Kearny on the main Platte River. He sent an express to Fort Pierre calling for five companies to meet him on the White River. Proceeding west along the Oregon Trail, making ten to twenty-five miles a day, Harney's troops found the marching fairly easy. Except for occasional heavy rains, the troops did well, and their spirits were high. After 190 miles they reached Ash Hollow.

They arrived there at 5:00 p.m., September 2, and could see fires from an Indian village to the northwest across the North Platte River. Using a spy glass, one of Harney's officers could see lodges in the distance. The command descended upon Ash Hollow, which was about 200 yards wide and 450 feet deep at that point. The day had been misty, and a moderate wind prevailed from the northeast, but by evening it was out of the southeast.

The soldiers made camp about 10:00 p.m. and Harney spent the night preparing an attack for the next day. About 3:00 a.m., Harney ordered the dragoons under Lieutenant Colonel Philip St. George Cooke to leave camp and detour over the table land of Blue Water Creek to be in position to intercept and attack the Indians from the north. With scout Joe Tesson in the lead, they crossed the North Platte and swung east of the village to encircle the unsuspecting Indians.

After about five miles, Cooke turned west toward the Blue Water Creek. To his surprise, he discovered another village, which he judged was about three miles above the main Indian camp. Luckily the dragoons were not detected, so they continued their march, finding a favorable position behind a slight ridge close to the village. Cooke later estimated they traveled ten or twelve miles, taking two hours to accomplish the sweep as it was almost daylight. From his vantage point, Cooke observed that a great force of Indians had gathered under a rugged bluff across the valley, about three-quarters of a mile below his command.

In the meantime, Harney had broken camp at 4:30 a.m. and, with five companies under the immediate command of Major Albermarle Cady, crossed the river and proceeded toward the Indian village "with a view to attacking openly in concert with the cavalry." Not until after the fight did Harney learn that trader Jim Bordeaux had sent a Brulé called Goose to warn of the soldiers' approach. The Indians, however, decided to stay because the buffalo hides and meat they were drying were still too green.

A woman and two children who were leading a pony toward the Indian camp before daylight heard the soldiers and gave the first alarm. Both parties were surprised and, not daring to wait for the infantry to attack, Cooke placed the dismounted light artillery in the front, keeping the mounted dragoons in position to pursue escaping Indians on either flank.

Seeing Harney's force advancing, the Indians decided to retreat. They began to strike the lodges and commenced a rapid flight up the valley. But Chief Little Thunder appeared in front of the troops carrying an umbrella, an acknowledged sign of truce. Accompanied by a man named Iron Shell, Little Thunder professed friendship for the white men and, although he did not wish them harm personally, said he would be unable to deliver the parties responsible for the Grattan Massacre. He also confessed he had no control over the young men, and it would be best if the soldiers left.

Harney curtly ended the parley by telling the chief that "his people had depradated upon and insulted our citizens whilst moving quietly through the country, that they had massacred troops and now the day of retribution had come!"

While Little Thunder rode back to tell his people what Harney said and to prepare to fight, Captain J.B. Todd's Company A of the 6th Infantry moved out in front of the troops as skirmishers. Harney ascertained the enemy was within range, then gave the order to fire.

Todd's troops opened fire, slowly driving the warriors toward Cooke. The fight almost immediately turned into a rout as Indian arrows and old rusty flintlocks proved inadequate against the well-armed soldiers. The light artillery company under a Captain Howe dismounted and fought the Indians on foot; after a short struggle they drove the Indians from their position. The

Indians fell back to the foot of a hill where their horses were concealed. They mounted and rode north, pursued by the dragoons. They retreated through a gap in the range of hills bordering the river on the south, and fell back about three miles where they took up a strong position along the base of a rugged bluff. Harney stood atop the highest hill so he could overlook the operations.

The soldiers found the hill facing the river to be a rotten limestone formation filled with little caves and overgrown by a dense undergrowth which hid the cave openings. They soon learned the Indians were in the caves and were offering resistance.

The artillery moved in and blasted the caves for several minutes, until soldiers heard the cry of a child; word then went down the line that women and children were concealed in the caves and behind the rocks. Orders were given to cease fire, giving two Indians a chance to escape. However, twelve warriors had been killed and, after several moments, the surviving women and children surrendered.

Retired Adjutant General R.C. Drum, who was a first lieutenant with Company G, 4th U.S. Artillery at Ash Hollow, gave his personal account in 1911. "On our return from reinforcing Captain [William] Steele," said the general, "riding down the steep hill from General Harney's headquarters, I saw a disturbance in the deep grass just ahead and said to the officer with me that there [were] Indians hiding and if he would make a rapid movement to the right I would make a dash for the object. He did so and I made a rush but only found a little child, naked, excepting a scarf around its waist, in which was a little puppy dog. I told the sergeant to pick it up, and as he did so…[the child] scratched a bit like a wildcat. Having a lemonade in my canteen with a little whiskey, and knowing the mollifying effects of the decoction on Indian temper, I handed it to the sergeant to give the waif a sip, which had a happy effect."

The fight was over in a short time with the Indians suffering a crushing blow. Harney found forty-one Brulé lodges in the lower camp and eleven Oglala lodges in the upper camp. Assuming there were two warriors and a total of seven people in each lodge, the estimated number of Indians present totaled 364, including 104 warriors. Harney reported eighty-six Indians killed, five wounded, and seventy women and children captured. Harney lost two men and seven were wounded.

Little Thunder, suffering two terrible sabre wounds, escaped on an abandoned dragoon horse. Spotted Tail, who was soon to become a famous Sioux chief, was also badly wounded. Although he managed to escape, his wife and child were captured.

Soldiers spent the rest of the day gathering materials the Indians left behind. Those were brought in by wagon and burned. The expedition left for Fort Laramie on September 9, but not before throwing up a twenty-by-forty foot sod redoubt with a roof and square potholes; they named it Camp Grattan.

Did Harney and his men commit atrocities that day? In his December 3rd report, Secretary of War Jefferson Davis said, "papers and property captured at Ash Hollow leave no doubt that this band concerned in the [Grattan] massacre." Remnants of clothing were found that had apparently been carried off in the Grattan incident. That does not mean, however, that a peaceful settlement could not have been reached with Little Thunder's band.

Looking across Blue Creek into the rough terrain where the Indians fled. Those who were not killed or captured escaped to the the left of the photo, into the Sandhills out of Harney's reach.
(Photo June 1929 by Emil Kopac, Oshkosh, Nebraska)

There is no doubt that Harney was interested in a military solution to the problem, not a negotiated one.

At first the public hailed Harney as a hero. He had done a great job on the North Platte River, giving the Indians who had committed many atrocities their comeuppance. Only after stories of the affair had been related did the public become incensed over the "Harney Massacre." One account had Harney ordering the Indians to retire fifty paces—then killing the men, women and children.

Harney became known as a "Squaw Killer," a label that would haunt him the rest of his days. General Winfield Scott believed Harney was careless in regard to the women and children and said so publicly.

Undoubtedly, Harney gave no quarter to the adult male Indians who fought ferociously. It is also a fact that some women and children were killed in the fight, and only the men who fought there that day could have said whether or not they deliberately slaughtered innocent Indians. Many of those casualties resulted from fire directed at the armed hostiles in the rock shelters or in open sight when distance and dress prevented recognition of sex and age differences.

Nevertheless, the expedition got results. Throughout November, various bands, such as the Minneconjou and Sans Arcs, came in; Indian leaders Spotted Tail, Red Leaf, and Long Chin also surrendered.

Harney brought the campaign to a close. Although convinced the Indians were in a sorry state and wanted peace to avoid being killed or starved, he knew there would be more trouble the next spring. Prophetically, he said, "I fear they will divide into small groups and we'll have another Florida War on our hands; then it will be for the Indians to fix the time for peace. On this immense frontier the Indians, if they adopt that policy, will be capable of incalculable mischief."

The Scalping of William Thompson

One of the most dangerous jobs in the West during the 1860s was that of maintaining track for the Union Pacific Railroad along the Platte River in Nebraska. Men who worked on the tracks had to withstand 100-degree heat in the summer and five-below-zero cold in the winter while working on the windswept prairies of central and western Nebraska.

If the elements were not enough to try a man's courage and patience, roving bands of Sioux and Cheyenne braves would swoop down unexpectedly from the Sandhills and return to the Pine Ridge or Black Hills with fresh scalps tied to their belts.

Mostly Irish, these workers provided the labor needed to keep the trains moving. Once track was laid, small wooden shacks, called section houses, were built at regular intervals along the railroad tracks for these hardy men to live in. Each section house was manned by five to seven workers. Led by a section foreman, they were in charge of maintaining about six miles of track.

One hot, humid night in early August of 1867, this job proved to be not only dangerous, but also deadly for the Irishmen at Plum Creek Station, which is now Lexington, Nebraska. On that night, Turkey Leg, a sub-chief of the Southern Cheyenne, chose to accomplish what few plains Indians were ever able to do: derail a train. Well known to the military, Turkey Leg was bent on making sure the white man paid for building the railroad through Indian Territory. He would be involved in several skirmishes with the military within a short period of time.

On the evening of August 6, 1867, at 7:30 p.m., telegraph operator Samuel D. Wallace noticed that all communication west of Plum Creek Station had abruptly stopped. Finding this odd, Wallace walked the short distance to the nearby section house, hoping to find the crew there. He was in luck; the section crew had just returned from a full day of making repairs to the track four miles west of Plum Creek, and were wearily sitting around the shack.

Wallace approached Section Foreman James Delahunty about the break in communication and asked that he check it out. Delahunty acknowledged Wallace and told the crew to get ready for they would have to go back out, find the trouble and, if possible, repair it. After a hurried supper, Delahunty, Tim Murphy, Patrick Handerhand, Patrick Griswold, and William Thompson grabbed their tools and rifles and climbed aboard a handcar. None of them suspected that renegade Southern Cheyenne warriors, led by Chief Turkey Leg, had cut the telegraph line and were prepared to derail an "Iron Horse."

The spot the Cheyenne chose to set up for the derailment was well-scouted, directly west from Plum Creek, where, for several miles, the tracks ran in a relatively straight line. At that point, about three-and-a-half miles west of the station, the tracks curved to the northwest. The Indians chose the spot carefully, because no one could see the tracks very far ahead due to the curve. In additon, it was almost dark when they left, and the Indians had prepared an almost perfect ambush. Ironically, they used tools left by previous railroad workers to build the trap. Using the telegraph wire cut from the line paralleling the railroad, the Cheyenne attached a tie directly under the end of the rails which had been pried up into the air.

The section crews' eyes were glued on the telegraph line as they sped toward disaster. Nearing the location for the ambush, the crew suddenly saw Indians in the light of fire flickering on the north side of the tracks, causing them to slow down. Delahunty ordered the crew to keep pumping the handcar since he was familiar with the area. Unfortunately, in the deepening dusk, no one on the handcar saw the large tie lying on the rails up in front of them.

Going at full speed, the handcar struck the tie with a tremendous impact. Lurching crazily off the tracks, it threw the men and their gear into a nearly dry creek bed. Before they knew what had happened, Turkey Leg and twenty-five mounted warriors were upon them. Each man scrambled for his weapon, opened fire on the attacking Indians, and then began running back toward Plum Creek Station. Handerhand, Griswold, and Thompson didn't have a chance. They were cut off from the other men by the hostile charge.

The Indians rode in close to the desperate trio and struck Handerhand to the ground with their war clubs. Griswold, shot through the hip, managed to elude the

Indians by crawling off into the darkness to safety. Thompson evaded his pursuers for a short distance, but was run down by a mounted Cheyenne who shot him through one arm and knocked him down with his rifle. Quickly, the Cheyenne was on top of him. Placing his knee on Thompson's back, he grabbed the man's hair and according to Thompson himself, "making a twirl round his fingers with my hair he commenced hacking and sawing away at my scalp."

Playing dead while the Indian finished the grisly task of tearing off his scalp, Thompson watched the Indian hop onto his pony and trot away. Strangely enough, the brave dropped the scalp a short distance away and rode off into the night. Thompson crawled over, grabbed his bloodied scalp, and watched as the Cheyenne worked on the barrier of rails and ties.

Delahunty and the rest of the crew were able to shoot two Cheyenne and a pony while running back to Plum Creek. This was enough to discourage their pursuers, and the railroaders made good their escape. Unfortunately, none of them were in a position to warn the fast-coming approaching freight from the east.

The engineer of this freight train, Brooks Bowers, seeing the Indians approaching in the firelight, opened the throttle and tried to outdistance their horses. Bowers then saw the dumped handcar and pulled hard on the brakes, but it was too late. The cars behind, flatcars loaded with bricks, and trailing at twenty-five miles per hours, humped up on the tender, driving the engine into the obstacle on the tracks. Fireman George Henshaw slammed into the firebox and was killed instantly. Bowers was thrown out of the window by the impact, also mortally wounded.

The four men in the caboose which, along with thirteen other cars that had somehow been able to remain on the tracks, were shaken. Conductor William Kinney, brakeman Fred Lewis, and firemen Charles Radcliffe and F.L. Barker had been thrown to the caboose floor when the train hit the barrier. The men staggered out of the wrecked car and viewed the scene around them. Kinney, realizing that a second freight train was right behind, grabbed his lantern and raced back up the right-of-way to flag it down. The other three men stumbled off into the darkness and spent the next two nights on a Platte River sandbar, frightened but safe.

Kinney was able to flag down the second train and back it up to Plum Creek Station. A telegraph message was sent east to Omaha detailing the wreck. After picking up the terrified residents of Plum Creek, the train backed up to Elm Creek. Only two men remained in Plum Creek that night—Dan Freeman and Patrick Delahunty. Freeman was worried about leaving his store, and Pat Delahunty volunteered to help guard it, saying, "Give us a gallon of whiskey and plenty of bullets and we'll be here in the morning."

News of the train wreck crackled up and down the telegraph wire. Not long after the second train pulled into Plum Creek, Delahunty, Murphy, and Kearn also arrived. Pat Griswold staggered in sometime later, reporting that Handerhand and Thompson were dead.

This was the news that Union Pacific officials had long dreaded. Months earlier, when Sioux and Cheyenne were running roughshod over the construction crews, Chief Engineer Grenville Dodge had written to General William T. Sherman, Commander of the Platte. "...We cannot hold our men to our work unless we have troops. Our men will not stay at their tanks and stations twenty miles apart, unprotected...I tremble every day for fear of a stampede. State agents, telegraph men, emigrants, tie constructors, and railroad men of all descriptions out there are pressing for protection."

Meanwhile, back at the wreck, a hurting Thompson watched as the Indians scalped Bowers and then broke into the remaining boxcars full of tools, foodstuffs, clothing, bolts of calico, rifles, cartridges, and whiskey. The Indians got drunk, dressed up in velvet, calico, and silk, then spent the rest of the night dancing around the bonfire. They set the boxcars on fire, throwing the bodies of Bowers and Henshaw into the flames. Thompson, who had been lying motionless since being scalped, decided this was the time to escape. He crawled and walked along the tracks to the Willow Island Depot, almost fifteen miles to the west.

A company of Major North's Pawnee Scouts were called in from Fort McPherson near North Platte, and another company sent from Omaha under his brother, Luther. The railroad men, too impatient to wait for the Pawnee Scouts, climbed aboard a special train on the morning of the 7th and headed for the crash scene. When the impromptu force reached Plum Creek, they saw smoke billowing in the distance. A flatcar was pushed in front of the engine and fortified with ties, the heavily armed men setting up a make-shift fort.

Proceeding to the derailment location, they spotted Cheyenne galloping across the prairie, colorful rolls of calico streaming from their horses. Others had cracked open boxes of boots and cut the bottoms off, using the tops for leggings as they danced around the smoldering fire.

From the flatcar, Delahunty picked off an Indian with his Spencer carbine. This quickly encouraged the Indians to leave the area. Grabbing what loot they could carry, the victorious Cheyenne broke for the hills south of the tracks. The train eased to the crash scene, and a couple of men made a dash to the engine, looking for Bowers. All they were able to find were the immolated bodies of Bowers and Henshaw.

A short time later, North's Pawnee Scouts arrived at Plum Creek from North Platte aboard a special train, unloaded horses and at once took off after the Cheyenne. Turkey Leg's band was far out in front, however, and the Pawnee gave up after a short chase. Work crews then moved in to clear the tracks. Thompson and the bodies of Bowers and Henshaw were placed on a passenger train for Omaha.

Henry M. Stanley, the famous English correspondent well known for finding Dr. Livingstone in Africa, happened to be in Omaha when the train arrived. He wrote, "The bodies, or what was left of them, were in two boxes, approximately 12" by 30". For the benefit of the public, one box was opened. There, surrounded by cotton, lay a charred trunk about two feet in length resembling a half burnt log..."

People flocked from everywhere to see Thompson, more dead than alive, arrive holding a bucket of salt water containing his scalp. Stanley reports, "to view the gory baldness which had come so suddenly upon him fascinated the local populace...Thompson was quite weak, which was not surprising what with a bullet hole through one arm, a knife wound in the neck, and the top of his head gone."

William Thompson after surviving the Indian attack.
(Nebraska State Historical Society)

A local surgeon, Dr. R.C. Moore, stitched the scalp into place, but the operation did not succeed. Stanley, who had peered into the bucket containing the scalp, said the patch of skin was about nine inches long and four inches wide, somewhat resembling a drowned rat, as it floated curled up in the water.

Thompson returned home to his native England with his scalp which, by then, had been tanned. For some unexplained reason, he mailed it back to Dr. Moore, who gave it to the Omaha Public Library. For many years it was displayed there in a jar of alcohol. Only recently did the Library give the scalp to the Union Pacific Railroad Museum in Omaha, where it remains today. William Thompson died April 1894, in Milburn, England.

On May 28, 1940, a monument dedicated to the events of August 6-7, 1867, was erected by the Lexington, Nebraska, D.A.R. chapter. A plaque was mounted on an eight-ton granite boulder donated by the Union Pacific Railroad. A special guest on that day was Clinton

U. Bowers, son of the engineer, Brook Bowers, who was killed in the incident. Mr. Bowers was just two years old at the time, and one of four children orphaned by the tragedy. He brought the casket plate from his father's coffin for the commemoration.

Today, only the stone monument four miles west of Lexington, Nebraska, and William Thompson's scalp at the Union Pacific Museum in Omaha, Nebraska, remain to remind today's travelers of the days when the road west across Nebraska wasn't quite so tame.

How Philip Wells Lost His Nose

Wounded Knee Creek 1890

Judge Eli S. Ricker, rancher, attorney, and newspaperman in northwest Nebraska during the late 19th century, spent the better part of twenty-five years interviewing retired military personnel, scouts, packers, and Indians on or near the Pine Ridge Sioux Indian Reservation. In fact, he conducted over two hundred interviews written on children's Chief tablets that his family turned over to the Nebraska State Historical Society at the time of his death in 1926. These interviews are invaluable because they are from primary sources—men who experienced life in the Old West during the Indian wars.

Many of these interviews deal with what happened at Wounded Knee in 1890. On the morning of December 29, 1890, near a creek named Wounded Knee in South Dakota, the Seventh Cavalry of the United States Army commanded by Colonel James W. Forsyth, attempted to disarm a Sioux Indian village. Its residents were followers of Big Foot and the recently slain Sitting Bull. They had escaped arrest and fled from the north to the protection of their Pine Ridge kinsmen, until they were inter-

Judge E.S. Ricker of Chadron, NE. Taken in 1916 at the age of 73.
(Nebraska State Historical Society)

cepted the day before by the soldiers and escorted to a campsite along the Wounded Knee.

That morning, Forsyth attempted to disarm the Indians resulting in a terrible massacre in which almost two hundred Sioux men, women, and children were killed with many others wounded. A man named Philip Wells was employed as interpreter by the United States Army under Forsyth's command. Wells was a participant in the events of that fateful day. He related those events to Judge Ricker in 1906. This story is based on that interview.

"Wells was appointed Assistant Clerk at the Pine Ridge Indian Reservation in 1887 and in 1889 served as the official interpreter for the Sioux Commission. In the fall of 1890, he resigned to take a position as chief of scouts and interpreter for Forsyth's Seventh Cavalry.

"Wells takes up his story on the morning all of the Indians had been summoned to give up their arms. They congregated in the middle of the camp, surrounded on all sides by United States soldiers. As Forsyth and Wells walked among the Indians, a medicine man began to address the Indians.

"Forsyth turned away while Wells watched and listened to the medicine man on the west side of the circle hold up his arms in supplication and prayer for protection. Forsyth asked Wells what the Indian was saying. Wells replied impatiently that, 'It is nothing but a harmless prayer, Colonel, but don't disturb me, for I must pay very close attention to catch all he means. I will let you know just as soon as he says anything you should know.' Forsyth nodded his head and walked away.

"Suddenly, the Indian stopped praying and, stooping down, took some dirt and rose up facing west. He raised his two hands, and still facing west, cast the dirt in a circular motion toward the soldiers. Then he walked around the circle. When he returned to the starting point, he stopped and uttered exclamations in Sioux which signified regret, and his decision on a desperate course. For instance, if he had submitted to abuse, insults, or wrong with patience and fortitude, he has made up his mind to retaliate or take revenge upon the offender, he exclaims, 'Haha! Haha! I have lived long enough.'

"Then, a medicine man named Sits Straight turned to the young men who were standing together and said, 'Do not be afraid and let your hearts be strong to see what is before you; we are well aware that there are lots of soldiers about us and that they have lots of bullets; but I have received assurance that their bullets cannot penetrate us. The prairie is large and the bullets will not go toward you, but over the large prairie, and if they do go towards you, they will not penetrate you. As you saw one throw up the dust and it floated away, so will the bullets float away harmlessly over the prairie.'

"Wells saw Big Foot's brother-in-law and stepped over to him with the intention of convincing him to quiet and pacify the Indians. Just then, Colonel Forsyth called to him saying he better get out of there for it was beginning to look dangerous. Wells replied, 'In a minute, Colonel, I want to see if I can't get this fellow to quiet them.' Wells turned back to the Indian and said, 'Friend, go in among the young men and quiet them, talk to them as a man of your age should.' He talked in a low voice so that the Indians could not hear. The Indian replied, very loud so that all the Indians could hear his words, 'Why, friend, your heart seems to beat. Who is talking of trouble or fighting?'

"Wells spoke, 'Yes, friend, my heart beats when I see so many helpless women and children if anything should happen.'

"'Friend, it is unnecessary that your heart should beat,' again the Indian said loudly. As he spoke, a powerfully built Sioux man stepped out of the circle and came around to where Wells and the older Indian were standing. He stepped slowly as though he intended to get behind Wells without the interpreter observing what he was doing.

"Wells suspected his purpose and watched him closely. As the young Indian moved closer, Wells kept turning his own body so the warrior could not get behind him. At the same time, seeing that he could not persuade the older Indian, he continued to talk, attempting to change the subject. Wells held his rifle with both hands at the muzzle, the butt resting on the ground. It appeared that the young Indian didn't have a rifle under his blanket, but Wells could not tell if he had a revolver or a knife concealed.

"Wells reflected on the different modes of attack which the Indian might be contemplating; whether he would grapple and try to overpower him; whether he would strike him with a club or knife; or whether he would use some other manner to kill him and get his gun. He dared not turn his back on him, but began to move backwards; when he got far enough from him to walk away to safety, he intended to get out of the circle.

"By this time, Wells was convinced a clash was coming. At that instant, Wells heard a cry, 'Look out! Look out!' coming from the his rear and left. He threw his rifle into the 'port' position and turned his head quickly to the left and rear for a look at the Indians standing in a circle. He saw one Indian near the center of the circle facing the soldiers with his gun pointed at an upward angle—the last position in which a hunter holds his piece before placing it to his shoulder to fire. Then the gun was discharged over the soldiers' heads, the smoke drifting upwards. Suddenly, five or six young warriors threw off their blankets and drew their guns. Wells heard the command which sounded like Forsyth's voice yell out, 'Fire! Fire on them!'

"Wells, thinking of the Indian near him, turned toward him, both movements occupying only an instant of time. The Indian came upon him with a raised butcher knife ground to a sharp point and attempted to deal him a deadly blow.

"Wells dropped to one knee while at the same time, throwing up his rifle with both hands as a guard, and ducked his head to avoid a blow in the face. The Sioux's wrist struck the gun, but the knife was long enough to reach Well's nose which was nearly severed. It hung down over his mouth by a thin strip of skin. Before Wells could rise, the Indian renewed his attack, standing over him with the savage knife uplifted and tried to grasp the rifle with his left hand. It was a desperate play between life and death and lasted but a moment. Wells held the rifle above his head, keeping it in swift motion as a guard against the knife. The Indian summoned all his strength to break down Well's guard with a furious blow using the weight of his body. He raised the blade higher in the air for the mighty stroke, but in the process let down his guard, and Wells struck him with the rifle. The Indian staggered backwards, momentarily stunned.

"Wells leveled his rifle at the Indian's breast and threatened to fire. Anticipating the shot, the Indian made a quarter turn and dropped on his hands and knees. Like a flash, the rifle went down and Wells pulled the trigger, the bullet entered the Indian's side below the arm. He pitched forward on his face, dead. A soldier rushed up to the prostrate body, placed the muzzle of his own gun between the Indians shoulder blades and fired. At the same instant, a bullet struck the soldier inflicting a mortal wound.

"Wells started for shelter behind a nearby wagon. Running along, he slipped on the snow and nearly fell. A young brave who was chasing him, dealt a blow with his knife from behind, intending to stab him in the back. Luckily, he overreached and cut Well's coat instead.

"Wells remained in action until the main fight was over. Whenever he took aim with his rifle, the piece of his nose suspended by the skin got in the way, Several times he tried to pull it off, but was unsuccessful. Wells always felt that it worked out better in the long run that

Lieutenant Taylor and seven of his Indian scouts, Pine Ridge Agency, January 19th, 1891. (*South Dakota Historical Society*)

he couldn't get it off, since it was replaced by a surgeon and he used it for a good many years afterwards.

"Wells did offer his opinion to Ricker regarding Big Foot's intentions:

"'I do not believe they had any intention of fighting, and for these reasons: First, when Major Whiteside met Big Foot at Porcupine Butte, Big Foot was drawn up in battle array and was perhaps equal to Whiteside in numbers.

"'Second, the ground was in his favor, being adapted to the Indian style of fighting, whereas, the soldiers would have had, for awhile at least, to operate in the open plain.

"'Third, after the Indians knew they were discovered and the troops were coming, the Indians had ample time for defensive preparations and did not improve the opportunity to make themselves more impregnable.

"'When Whiteside met them, he formed his troops in line of battle. While in these positions, a long parley took place. If the Indians had not been willing to yield, they could have safely retreated with the landscape favoring their movements and their rear guard fighting.

"'Fourth, but the Indians had surrendered. When they came to Wounded Knee, they were prisoners in possession of their arms. The battle there was over the question of giving up the guns. Big Foot admitted the principle which Forsyth contended; namely, that the Indians should surrender their weapons, but used evasion to avoid doing so. The Indians delivered before the action only some inferior pieces.'

"Wells believed the Indians put up a bluff, but it got out of control—it was carried too far—till the young warriors plunged over the danger line and precipitated the tragedy. He told Ricker that after the action, he stood by the dead body of Big Foot's brother-in-law and, after Indian custom, addressed the dead man, 'Haha!' the Indian exclamation of regret. 'Friend, I tried to save you, but you would not obey me, and now you have destroyed yourself.' At that, the wounded Indians lying within hearing, uttered their approval of what he said, by the usual, 'How.' They had heard him in conversation with the man before the battle and knew from the Indian's answers that Wells was pleading with him to pacify the people."

Dewey Beard

Indian Survivor of Wounded Knee

This interview about the Battle of Wounded Knee was given to Judge Eli Ricker at Day School No. 29, Pine Ridge Reservation on February 20, 1907—Joseph Horn Cloud—Interpreted by Dewey Beard, age forty-three. His story begins one morning in December 1890. Big Foot's people have been summoned to a council and instructed they must turn in all their weapons. They are surrounded by soldiers. The Indians are nervous and uneasy and the troops are ready for action. As you read this interview, please note the viewpoint fluctuates between Dewey Beard and Judge Ricker.

Dewey says...

"All the Indians came to the center for the council. Two lines of foot soldiers stood immediately around the Indians. Another two ranks of soldiers encircled the Indian camp, the last rank being mounted. There was a council. I stayed inside my lodge—did not go to the council; had a notion to start with the wagons. While I was in my tent, my mother came and looked in and said, 'My son, some soldiers are coming and gathering all the guns, powder, axes, knives, bows and arrows and they are coming this way.'

"When I looked out, I saw soldiers coming loaded with guns, knives, axes, crowbars, war clubs, bows and arrows. I saw all this with my own eyes. I went inside and got my carbine gun and dug a little hole and laid my gun in and covered some dirt over it and threw the quilts and blankets over to the other side of the lodge (not over the covered gun—Ricker note). A soldier came and looked in and told him to come to the council. Before doing so, he took some cartridges and buried them outside his lodge, in front of the door covering them with manure, so that if while at council trouble started, he would know where to find ammunition.

"While I was going to the council with the soldier, I passed my brother Joseph who was leaving the council, and I asked Joe what he was coming out of the council for, and he replied that he was going after water. I went into the council and saw ten young men standing a little to one side, these had given up their guns and belts and knives.

"While I was sitting in the council, my father came to me and admonished me to remember what he had said this morning. Then he asked me where my brothers were, and I answered, 'Two of them were standing over among those ten men,' and father added that we ought to stay together.

"Then one of the interpreters said, 'This officer asked yesterday for 25 guns, but you did not give them, now he will get them, he will take them himself; so he will pick them himself and you better give those you have in your blankets, and your knives and belts and it will be all right. When you give all the guns and knives, you will stand in one rank right along the edge of this bank (meaning the ravine) and some number of soldiers will stand in front of you and aim the guns at your foreheads, but the guns are unloaded.' Joe explains that the Indians were to submit to this in the nature of penance, admitting thereby that in not turning over the guns the day before, they had done wrong and would submit to this nonsense in order to wipe away their fault.

"The Indians did not understand the soldier's orders. They could not comprehend this foolishness. But this offended and angered them and they reasoned among themselves and said they were human beings and not cattle to be used this way. They said they did not want to be killed like dogs. We are people in this world.

"Most of the Indians had given up their arms; there were a few standing with their guns, but the soldiers had not been to them. The knives were piled up in the center of the council; some young men had their guns and knives, but they had not been asked yet for them.

"There was a deaf Indian named Black Coyote who did not want to give up his gun; he did not understand what they were giving up their arms for. The Indians agreed among themselves that they would explain to him what the disarming meant, and then they would take his gun away from him. The Indians who had so agreed wanted to tell the officers of their plan, but the interpreter was gone just then, and Horned Cloud asked where the interpreter was. The people were getting excited. Nobody said anything in answer to Horned Cloud. The people grew wild. The deaf man heard about having guns pointed at their foreheads, and he said that he did not want to be killed, he was a man and was raised in this world.

"While the deaf man held his gun up, Beard could not hear all that was said on account of the confusion, but some soldiers came behind him and tried to take his gun from him. All the sergeants stepped back and yelled, 'Look out! Look out!' and held their guns toward the deaf man.

"While the two or three sergeants came to the deaf man and were struggling with him for possession of the gun, Dewey heard something on the west side and looked that way and saw the Indians were all excited and afraid, their faces changed as if they were wild with fear; he saw that the guns of the soldiers were pointed at the council, a part of whom were sitting down and few who were standing up. The older people had wrapped their blankets around their legs and were smoking. The struggle for the gun was short, the muzzle pointed upward toward the east and the gun was discharged.

"In an instant a volley followed as one shot, and the people began falling. He saw everybody was rolling and kicking on the ground. He looked southeastward and he did not know what he was going to do. He had only one knife. He looked eastward and saw the soldiers were firing on the Indians and stepping backwards and firing. His thought was to rush on the soldiers and take a gun from one of them. He rushed toward them on the west to get a gun. While he was running, he could see nothing for the smoke; through rifts he could see the brass buttons of the uniforms; he rushed up to a soldier whose gun rested over Dewey's shoulder and was discharged when the muzzle was near his ear and it deafened him for awhile.

"Then he grabbed the gun and wrenched it away from the soldier. When he got the gun, he drew his knife and stabbed the soldier in the breast, but the knife did not enter deep, and the soldier was trying to seize Dewey by the throat and by his buckskin coat about the breast; as the soldier raised his left arm, Dewey stabbed him again, this time in the side close to the heart. When the soldier fell down, he still kept struggling to rise, but Dewey got astraddle his body and held his head down and then stabbed him by the kidneys till he died. The soldier was crying as loud as he could. While Dewey was on this soldier, some other soldiers were shooting at him, but missed him and killed soldiers on the other side.

"When he got up he ran right through the soldiers toward the ravine, and he was the last Indian to go into the ravine. The soldiers were shooting at him from nearly all directions, and they shot him down. He fell down on his right arm, he began to rise up, and as he did so, he saw a soldier a few yards in front of him. The soldier began snapping his gun at him, but he was excited and probably his gun was not loaded, as it did not go off. Dewey Beard at length raised to his knees to shoot the soldier, he snapped, but he too had been in too much of a hurry and had not loaded his gun.

"Dewey tried to get to the ravine and succeeded in getting on his feet, as he was going, he met a soldier coming up out of the ravine. The soldier tried to go around him but could not and Dewey shot him in the breast and killed him. After the soldier fell, he was kicking and Dewey jumped over him to go on. Right on the edge of the ravine on the south side were soldiers shooting at the Indians who were running down into the ravine, the soldiers' shots sounded like firecrackers and hail in a storm; a great many Indians were killed and wounded down in there. While Dewey was going down into the ravine he was shot again, this time in the leg just above the knee; as he expresses it, 'in the lap.' He then sat down, got out his cartridges and shot at the soldiers right at the edge of the bank; doesn't know how many times he shot, but a good many. While shooting, a shell got stuck in his gun as he could not shoot it anymore. Then he ran a little farther up the ravine.

"When he went to the bottom of the ravine, he saw many little children lying dead in the ravine. He was now pretty weak from his wounds. Now when he saw all those little infants lying there dead in their blood, his feeling was that even if he ate one of the soldiers, it would not appease his anger. He went farther up the ravine and came to an old Indian who had a gun which he was holding up and he said to the old man, 'Give me that gun and you take this one,' and they exchanged. When he got the gun he made another rush at the soldiers, accompanied by two other Indians who got killed on the flat on the south side of the ravine.

"He now returned to the ravine alone. Just before he got to the edge of the ravine to go down into it, he met what at first he thought was a soldier, but it proved to be an Indian scout; the two shot at each other, but both missed his man. Just before he started down the ravine, but after shooting at the Indian scout, one of Big Foot's men grabbed him by the buckskin coat and swung himself behind Beard. The soldiers shot at the two men but missed Beard and killed the other man. The Indians all knew that Dewey was wounded, but those in the ravine wanted him to help them. So he fought with his life to defend his own people. He took his courage to do that—I was pretty weak and now fell down. A man who was wounded by being shot through the lower jaw, had a belt of cartridges which he offered Beard and asked him to try to help them again. When he gave me the cartridges, I told him I was badly wounded and pretty weak too. While I was lying on my back, I looked down the ravine and saw a lot of women coming up and crying. When I saw these women, girls and little girls and boys coming up, I saw soldiers on both sides of the ravine shoot at them until they had killed everyone of them. He saw a young woman among them coming and crying and calling, 'Mother! Mother!' She was wounded under her chin, close to her throat, and the bullet had passed through a braid of her hair and carried some of it into the wound, and then the bullet had entered the front side of her shoulder and passed out the backside.

"Dewey was sitting up and he called to her to come to him. When she came close to him, she fell to the ground. He caught her by the dress and drew her to him across his legs. When the women who the soldiers were shooting at got a little past him, he told the girl to follow them on the run, and she went up the ravine. He got himself up and followed up the ravine. He saw many dead men, women, and children lying in the ravine. When he went a little way up, he heard singing; going a little farther, he came upon his mother who was moving slowly, being badly wounded. She had a soldier's revolver in her hand, swinging it as she went. Dewey does not know how she got it. When he caught up to her she said, 'My son, pass by me; I am going to fall down now.'

As she went up, soldiers on both sides of the ravine shot at her and killed her.

"I returned fire upon them, defending my mother. When I shot at the soldiers in a northern direction, I looked back at my mother and she had already fallen down. I passed right on from my dead mother and met a man coming down the ravine who was wounded in the knee. Now these two men were the targets for many rifles on both sides of the ravine. Hundreds of bullets threw dirt and dust around them. The wounded man had a Winchester rifle and he offered it to Beard and asked him to kill as many as he could, but Beard did not take the Winchester. A little while before this he had gotten rid of the disabled gun in which the shell stuck; he had given it to White Lance's partner and taken one from him; these guns were some taken from soldiers. We didn't have any guns of our own; all these guns we had taken from soldiers to defend ourselves with. We took the guns not from dead soldiers, but from living ones; all of us young men took them.

"Afterwards, having used all the cartridges for the carbine he had, he now took the Winchester from the old man who said there were a good many cartridges inside of it. When he took this, he heard more noise of shooting up the ravine. He heard someone say that White Lance (Dewey's brother) was killed. Dewey was wounded so that his right arm was disabled; he placed the thumb of his right hand between his teeth and carried his Winchester on his left shoulder, and then he ran towards where he had heard that White Lance had been killed.

"As he ran, he saw lots of women and children lying along the ravine, some alive and some dead. He saw some young men above, and these he addressed, saying to them to take courage and do all they could to defend the women. 'I have a bad wound and am not able to defend them; I cannot aim the gun,' and so he told the young men this way. It was now in the ravine just like a prairie fire when it reaches brush and tall grass and rages with new power; it was like hail coming down; an awful fire was concentrated on them now and nothing could be seen for the smoke. In the bottom of the ravine, the bullets raised more dust than there was smoke, so that they could not see one another.

"When Dewey came into the 'pit,' he saw White Lance on top of the bank, and was rolling down towards the brink to get down into the ravine. He was badly wounded and at first was half dead, but later revived from his injuries. When Dewey went into the 'pit,' he found his brother William Horn Cloud lying or sitting against the bank shot through the breast, but yet alive; but he died that night. Just when I saw my wounded brother William, I saw White Lance slide down the bank and stand by William. Then William said to White Lance, 'Shake hands with me, I am dizzy now.'

"While they had this conversation, Dewey said, 'My dear brothers, be men and take courage. A few minutes ago, our father told us this way, and you heard it. Our father told us that all people of the world born of the same father and mother, when any great tragedy or danger comes, it is better that all of them should die together than that they should die separately at different times, one by one.' Meaning that it is better for all of the same family to die at one time in front of their relations, between them and the enemy; it looks better for their bones to be piled together in defense of their own people—better than for the family to die separately, leaving some behind to mourn for those who had died or been killed singly and alone.

"White Lance and William shook hands. Then White Lance and Dewey lifted their brother up and stood him on his feet; then they placed him on White Lance's shoulder. White Lance was wounded in several places and weak from loss of blood, but he succeeded in bearing William to the bottom of the ravine. There he was put down upon the ground, leaning against the bank.

"Dewey said they now heard the Hotchkiss or Gatling guns shooting at them along the bank. Now there went up from these dying people a medley of death songs that would make the hardest heart weep. Each one sings a different death song if he chooses. The death song is expressive of their wish to die. It is also a requiem for the dead.

"At this time, I was unable to do anything more and I took a rest, telling my brothers to keep up courage. The cannon were pouring in their shots and breaking down the bank which were giving protection to the fighting Indians. The warriors had been shooting at the cannon on the hill and driving back the gunners. The soldiers were close to the edge of the bank and these kept up a continual fire on the Indians. The Hotchkiss had been shooting rapidly and one Indian got killed by it. His body was penetrated in the pit of the stomach by a Hotchkiss shell, which tore a hole through his body six inches in diameter. The man was insensible, but breathed for an hour before he expired.

"At the same time this man was shot, a young woman close to Dewey was shot between the shoulders. The bullet came near hitting him. He heard a laugh and she was smiling, all unconscious that she was wounded. The next moment, a young man was shot down right in front of this woman. When the man fell, his bows and arrows fell on the ground. Dewey told some of the young men to gather up the bow and arrows and use them again. Dewey said to them, 'Get the bow and arrows and shoot at them; the white people are afraid of arrows.'

"Just at this trying moment, Dewey's reason and recollection seemed to resume possession of him, and the sight of this wounded young woman recalled his thoughts to his own dear wife and little boy (25 days old) and his parents, not knowing their fate. He went up the ravine in search of them. He came on to a number of women and children hovering in a little pit for shelter from the infuriated soldiers who were all around, shooting at them. When he arrived there they were all wounded, but yet alive. In this same place was a young woman with a pole in hand and a black blanket on it. When she would raise it up, the soldiers would whistle and yell and pour volleys into it.

"One woman spoke to Dewey and told him to come in among them and help them. He answered that he would stay where he was and make a fight for them; and that he did not care if he got killed, for the infants were all dead now, and he would like to die among the infants. He had now regained some strength so he could hold his gun. He was peeping out for the soldiers who were lying down on their breasts. There was one within a short distance, and him he shot and killed.

"Dewey now lay down again in a little hollow on his breast. When he raised up for another view of the soldiers, they were approaching. He took a shot at one

101

Indians, Wounded Knee Canyon (Nebraska State Historical Society)

and brought him down wounded, and two other soldiers took hold of the fallen man to drag him away. (After the trouble was past, Dewey heard in the talking of the fight, some soldiers say that this wounded soldier begged them to take him back to the Indians, so they might kill him).

"Dewey laid down again in the little hollow and re-loaded his gun. The soldiers across from him were shooting at him while he was loading. While he was loading, he heard a horseman coming along the brink of the ravine—could hear the foot falls. This man as he came along, gave orders to the men which he supposed were to fire on the women in the pit for a fusillade was instantly opened on them.

"Dewey raised himself for a look at this horseman, and he was not sure that he had on a sword, but he had something swinging. Dewey took a shot at the man and he fell from the horse. This man was the one who had driven the soldiers up close to the bank. Dewey saw him hanging down from his horse after he was shot, and the soldiers were fleeing back when they saw this officer was shot. I was wanting to see how the officer fell, so he was raising up to look, when a bullet swept close to his ear, after it first struck the ground and threw dirt in his eyes as to blind him.

"The battle at this juncture was very hot. But for being blinded by the dirt, he could have now picked off a number of soldiers, as they were standing on the level ground and he was behind the bank in the hollow. A good many shots were now directed at him and he went down and moved along the ravine, thinking he was going down, but he was going up the ravine. The sun was going down; it was pretty near sundown. He saw lots of dead persons in the bottom as he passed up the ravine. All the cavalry were coming down the hill; they saw him and began shooting at him. There was an Indian scout pretty close who shot at Dewey several times.

"Dewey climbed the hill farther in a southwesterly direction. While going, he looked back down on cemetery hill and saw something shining like a glass, and several shots were taken at him, going clear over his head and raising little clouds of dirt behind him. While this was doing, he saw five Oglala Sioux on horseback. He called them, but they were afraid and ran away, but he kept calling them, but they all stood still and he came up to them. He went on with them a little ways and soon he met his brother Joseph coming toward them on

*White Lance,
Joseph Horn
Cloud, Dewey
Beard, brothers
in Indian
costumes. Dewey
is on the far right.*

(Nebraska State
Historical Society)

horseback. Dewey asked, 'Where are you going?' Joe answered, 'All my brothers and parents are dead and I have to go in and be killed, too; therefore I have come back.'

"Dewey said, 'You better come with us; don't go there; they are all killed there,' and the five Oglalas left these two brothers. Then Joe got off his horse and told Dewey to get on. Dewey was covered with blood. He mounted the horse and Joe walked along slowly. After a little, a mounted Indian relation came up behind them. The three went together over to White Clay Creek below the mission and into the hostile camp. When they arrived, the Indians flocked about them to look at them and to shake hands with them. When the people were done shaking hands with them, they were told that their two youngest brothers had been brought over there, and now these younger brothers were brought to Dewey and Joseph. These were Frank and Ernest. Dewey wondered how these two younger brothers had got out of the trouble and reached White Clay. Seven of them were saved from Wounded Knee—five brothers, one sister and Dewey's little infant.

"Seven of his family were lost, viz, Horned Cloud, Sr. and wife; two brothers, William and Sherman; Dewey's wife, Wears Eagle; Good or Pretty Woman (a woman who lived with the Horned Clouds and was one of the family and a cousin of Dewey).

"Ernest was young and ran many miles and through overexertion and exposure, contracted consumption and died twelve years after, was never well again; and Dewey's little infant, Wet Feet, died afterwards in the next March. This child was nursing its dead mother who was shot in the breast. It swallowed blood and from this, vomited and was never well, was always sick till it died.

"When the fighting began at Wounded Knee, the sun was just a little above the hills. He has never made so complete a statement of this affair to any person. Dewey was at this time twenty five years old."

The Nat and Robert Martin Story

Pinned Together By An Arrow

George Martin brought his family to a homestead on a tract of land about twelve miles north of Juniata, Nebraska, in 1862. It was almost two years later, in the fall, that the Sioux Indians began to bother the settlers by stealing their horses. Those incidents precipitated this remarkable story. In the *Hastings Daily Tribune* issue of October 20, 1921, Nathaniel "Nat" Martin related what happened.

"When we first came to this country, in the early summer the buffalo were so numerous that by the end of July what grass grew on the prairie had been eaten or tramped upon until there was not much left but bare earth. The buffalo would then move on farther north in search of greener pasture. Some of the low places along the Platte River bottom retained enough moisture so that the grass came out quickly and in a short time would make a very fair crop of hay. These low places were very scattering and sometimes it was necessary to go several miles from the homeplace before a sufficient supply of hay had been placed inside the stockade for the winter's use.

"There was always danger of an Indian attack when one was any distance from the home place, but when haying we always went in parties of several persons and always well armed. The Henry repeating rifle had just come into use and father had one, while the rest of our weapons were old fashioned muzzle loading rifles. During the haying time, the stockherders used to keep a pretty sharp lookout for danger signs and if they discovered at anytime evidence of Indians the ranch house was immediately notified.

"One summer, the summer being unusually hot and dry, we had to go farther from home for our hay supply than ever before, but we made and cured the hay and got most of it in the stockade without being molested by our Indian neighbors, and perhaps for that reason we relaxed our watchfullness. The last two loads were to be hauled and as everyone about the ranch was busy, and that it had been so long since they had seen Indian sign, that he would take the chance of taking us two boys, Bob and myself, and an extra team and get the two loads at the same time.

"After dinner, we started for the hay field, father taking the Henry rifle with him. He drove a team of fine black stallions and Bob and I had a yoke of oxen and a lead horse. We drove to the hay field about two miles south of the Platte River, put on the loads and bound them down securely with long rope so that the center of the load was hollow in case of an Indian attack we would have a breast work for protection.

"We started for home and had got within about half or three-quarters of a mile, keeping close together up to this time although nothing had shown up to indicate any danger. In fact, the herder reported at noon that he had seen no Indian sign for a month, so we felt pretty safe.

"Father drove on ahead so as to get his load inside and be ready to help us boys when we came up. He got only a short distance ahead when the horses began to show signs of uneasiness, and when he raised up to see what the cause might be, he saw nine Indians coming from the mouth of a nearby draw. He knew they meant business so he secured the lines and taking the Henry, he worked towards the back of the load so he could protect us boys as well as himself.

"The Indians made out for father first and began shooting at him. He fired from the depression in the hay made by the binding pole and wounded one Indian. With a second shot, he crippled one of the Indians' ponies just as the rider drew back his bow to shoot under the pony's neck at father.

"The pony was unable to hold up his head so that Indian gave up the battle and took off down the road to see what we boys were doing. When we saw him coming, we unhitched the oxen and untied the horse. After putting my brother up on the horse, I climbed up behind and we hid on the other side of a little knoll.

"In the meantime, the Indians continued after dad who was making heroic efforts to reach the house. He let the horses go and devoted all of his time to his gun. When the Indians heard him shoot a third time, they dropped back in surprise, as they were not used to a gun that would shoot more than twice, and they thought they had father cornered when the second shot was gone.

"One Indian followed and succeeded by getting behind the load, and shot an arrow home. It struck father, lying on his stomach in the hay, in the neck, slicing the jugular vein and lodging in the collar bone. By this time, they were close to the house and as the team tore past the door, father dropped off. The Indian followed him around the load and would have ended his life but for my sister, Elizabeth, who rushed out of the house with an old shotgun and drove him off.

"Mother dragged my father off to the house and seeing by the nature of his injury that he required prompt attention, resorted to swift first aid.

"She sewed up the gash in his jugular vein with a pin and ran to the barn after a horse hair which she twisted around and around the pin, thus closing the gaping wound and staunching the flow of blood.

"When the Indians found that the family at the house were armed, they fled back a way, except one, who swung in by the barn picking up my brother's herd pony and driving him towards the north. This gave him a view of our hiding place and he signaled the other Indians who were standing with their chief about one fourth mile south of the house.

"As soon as they saw us, they rushed in our direction, driving us about a half a mile away from the house. Then the old horse upon which we were riding refused to be driven away any further and turned toward home. She was the mother of two colts and she seemed to know that they were in danger—one of the colts' mothers had died and she had adopted it.

"The Indians seemed to want to drive us away, capture us without killing us and get our horse. One brave, thinking he could head off our mad rush toward the house by getting in front of us and yelling, got a little too close to our mare and she grabbed his pony by the nape of the neck and almost threw him in her blind fury.

"The Indian was loath to give us up and still did not want to harm us evidently, so he made one more attempt to head us off. This time, our horse grabbed his blankets and jerked. At the same time, I tried to grab his bow but we both failed and he swung around behind and began shooting.

"The first arrow lodged in my right elbow, wedging its head in between the bones of the joint and causing great pain. I grabbed at the shaft and broke it off before I thought, throwing it into the face of the Indian. The second entered my back just under the shoulder blade next to the backbone, went through the right lung, came

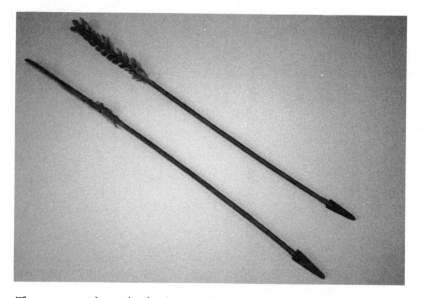

The arrow without the feathers is the one that pinned Nat and Robert Martin together. The other arrow was found at the site of the ambush. (Courtesy Hastings Museum)

out below the right breast and struck into Robert's backbone tight enough to hold us together.

"The third one grazed my hip inflicting a flesh wound and lodging in Robert's hip. Still we were rushing on toward the house as fast as the mare would go and that arrow shaft with its feathers working back and forth in my lung with each movement of the horse causing intense pain.

"I began to get faint and as I fell, I grabbed at Bob's waist band and pulled him with me. Bob was 11 years old and I was 14. We lay together where we fell and the mare plunged on towards the house. They finally captured her after she had become entangled in the long lines. The two Indians who had been after us the hardest came back to see if we were dead. They walked round and round, paying little attention to me since they thought that anyone with an arrow clear through him could not possibly live. They hit Bob on the head a number of times to be sure that he was finished and then one said, 'Shall we scalp them?'

"'Papoose scalp no good,' the other replied, 'No honor kill papoose.'

"According to the Indian idea of honor, it was a cowardly thing to kill a child and if a brave should bring in a scalp of anyone less than an adult, he would immediately be shunned and termed a 'squaw man.'

"The Indians finally departed, leading the mare in the direction of the house. Just before the boys fell, they saw their parents, standing on the top of the 'root house.'

"In falling, the arrow shaft pulled out of Nat's body and blood began spurting in great gushes from the wound. They lay still for a long time, afraid to move and almost too weak to do so, but finally Nat raised up on one elbow and said, 'Bob, are you dead? Bob!'

"Robert was just recovering consciousness and answered, 'No, I'm all right. Lay still. They're not gone yet.'

"After waiting some time, they crawled to the top of the knoll behind which they lay and looked toward their home. It was deserted. Both boys were suffering greatly and Nat had lost a great deal of blood which spurted with such force that it held his shirt from the wound. They were both soaked with blood from head to foot, but they were plucky.

"They crawled to the barn and found there a bed which the Indians had not torn up. It was in the side used by the colts which the Indians had taken with them, but the bed had been overlooked.

"Robert, the stronger of the two boys, went to the house to see if the family had been killed and found they had fled. Their house was on the stage line between Nebraska City and Fort Kearny and was used by travelers as a stopping place. Extra horses were kept in half of the barn. The front room of the house was called the 'Pilgrim Room,' where extra guests were made welcome and large stocks of provisions were stored. The Indians had taken what they wanted from this store room, slashing the bags which held the flour and grain. They had emptied everything into one great heap on the floor and mixed it all until the pile was nearly knee deep.

"Supper was almost ready and the Indians had eaten, showing dislike for the white man's coffee by kicking the pot outdoors. The team of stallions had been so frightened by the Indians who shot the boy's father that they had run up on a great woodpile in the backyard. The wagon was standing almost perpendicularly to the door of the house. The cut harness on the other side revealed that it had been necessary to release the team near the wagon so that it would not go over.

"The boys, weak from the pain and loss of blood, and frightened at being left alone, lay down on the bed in the barn and were mercifully granted unconsciousness."

After Mr. and Mrs. Martin saw their sons shot off the back of the faithful mother horse, they hastily prepared for a journey to Fort Kearny. The Martins thought the boys were dead. They were afraid of remaining on the ranch unguarded.

They took the horses which Mr. Martin cut loose from the load of hay and, with the women and the packs of food, they started on their long journey westward. Two of the Indians began to follow them. One of the team was shot by an Indian arrow after the family had gone only a short distance. It became necessary to abandon the horse, since it could no longer walk.

The next morning, the family decided to turn around and return to the ranch. A neighbor named Beck Martin, who wasn't related to the family, passed much of his time at the Martin ranch tending the stage horses, ran ahead of the others. He shaded his eyes with his hand, and looked into the window of the barn. Expecting to find his horses gone and the barn deserted, he was surprised to see the boys.

"'Here's the boys! Here's the boys!' his cry rang out.

It was only a second until every man in the party as well as the family were running as fast as they could go into the barn. Everyone was glad to see us. Mother and the girls couldn't run as fast as they did and when they arrived, the men cleared a way for them shouting, 'Here's the lady. Let her in.'

"Mother had arrived. She knelt beside us and immediately began to examine us for our wounds. I was so weak by that time that I could not raise my hand. We were both blood from head to foot but mother washed us off and did the best she could for us. She found the wound on my chest where the arrow had come out and said, 'Here's the wound.'

"'That's where it came out,' I told her.

"'Where it came out!' she exclaimed. 'Where did it go in?'

"I told her and they turned me over to see. She began to cry and said, 'Boy, you will die.' But I told her that I wasn't dead yet and I guess there was some hope.

"Then they found the string that held the arrowhead to the shaft I had broken off in my elbow. The arm was swollen so that the arrowhead was concealed.

"'Boy,' she said gently, 'that arrowhead will have to come out. It's right in the joint.'

"Dad got out the shoeing pincers and endeavored to pull it out. The pincers slipped and I lost consciousness. When I came to they tried it again and this time, after he got a good hold on it, two men held my arm while my father braced his feet on either side of the elbow and pulled. It measured four inches in length and they got it that time, but I didn't know anything until nine o'clock the next morning.

"When I woke up, they were trying to load me into the wagon and I was then ten miles from home—they had gone that far during the night on their way to Nebraska City, 169 miles away to get help from the nearest doctor.

"Every inch of me ached until I thought I could not stand the terrible jolting, but they said it was necessary and we went on. At the beginning of the third day of the journey, we had reached Beaver Crossing and I refused to be reloaded after passing the night in a deserted log cabin on the east bank of the stream. I was so sore that I begged them to go on and let me die. Father concluded to take me no farther.

"My brother suffered considerably but was able to get about. Father went back to Fort Kearny to try to get help from the soldiers but they refused. It was near the end of the Civil War and they would do nothing. Our horses were gone and so were our provisions.

"When father returned in about two weeks, we decided to go back on the ranch anyway and did so soon after. By that time I had sufficiently recovered to be able to sit up in a wagon seat, although I could neither get up or down.

"It was about a year before I was able to do any great amount of work owing to the great loss of blood. My brother had pain in his back much of the time for a number of years and his death in later life was due to spinal trouble which may have been the result of the injury he received."

Who Killed Tall Bull?

One of the most celebrated victories during the Indian Wars, at least at the time it was fought, was the Battle of Summit Springs on July 11, 1869. The *New York Times* splashed news of this victory across its front page. For years, Buffalo Bill Cody used a re-enactment of this fight in his Wild West Show. This fight is relatively unknown to people today, but it was, in fact, very exciting and even controversial.

The Republican River Expedition was organized for one purpose—to eliminate the hostile Cheyenne led by Tall Bull who were terrorizing the Republican River valley area in Colorado, Kansas, and Nebraska. Tall Bull's raids had been going on for several months. They attacked and destroyed farms from the Saline River in Kansas to the Big Sandy River in Nebraska. Between May 21 and May 28, they attacked a hunting party, derailed a Kansas Pacific train killing most of the crew, and raided a German emigrant settlement. During this raid, Tall Bull's Dog Soldiers killed thirteen German settlers and captured two white women—Mrs. Thomas Alderdice and her small baby, and Maria Weichel—in the raid on the Kansas settlement. Tall Bull's band had become a dangerous menace on the frontier and the time had come for someone to put a stop to their depredations.

General George A. Carr's 5th U.S. Cavalry, stationed at Fort McPherson, Nebraska, received orders on June 7th from the Department of the Platte in Omaha. He was to track down Tall Bull and eliminate his presence on the plains. Carr was an experienced frontier officer, described by one of his junior officers as a "master of methods of Indian warfare." Carr had fought well during the Civil War, accumulating a fine war record. Like hundreds of other officers left without commands after the great post-war demobilization, Carr had accepted a brevet rank with a reduced command rather than leave the army.

On June 9th, an expedition consisting of Carr's undermanned companies (400 men) and 150 Pawnee Scouts, led by Major Frank North and assisted by his brother Captain Luther North, left Fort McPherson and headed east along the Platte River. A young Buffalo Bill accompanied the group as a scout for the cavalry. It appears Cody showed early signs of a penchant for making money even at that time. Cody brought a wagon loaded with groceries, canned fruit, and vegetables to sell to the soldiers while in the field.

Luther North relates a humorous story about the first night out in the field.

A little before sundown Cody rode into camp and said he had to go back to the fort, and asked me to ride with him and have dinner at this house, and we would then come back to camp. I accepted his invitation and went with him. We had an excellent dinner and about ten or eleven o'clock started for camp. It was very dark and before we had gone two miles there came such a terrific storm of rain, hail and wind that our horses were about unmanageable. We kept on going, as we thought, in the direction of camp, but could see nothing. Finally the horses stopped and we could not get them to move any further.

I shouted to Cody that we had better wait for a flash of lightning so we could see where we were. When the flash came we found ourselves on the bank of a pond or slough, and neither knew where we were. The bank was perhaps ten feet high and if we had gone over it I do not know what would have become of us.

We waited till the storm was over and tried to figure out where we were but could not. Cody said, "Well, we're a pair of fine scouts, lost within three miles of the fort."

Luther North (second from right) at the location of Tall Bull's Lodge Summit Spring Fight, 1869. (Nebraska State Historical Society)

We stayed there until daylight, when we found the road that went on to camp. The boys (Pawnee Scouts) were just getting up and we told them we stayed at the fort overnight on account of the rain, and to the best of my recollection we never told anyone the truth.

Searching in vain for Tall Bull's band, the column marched over three hundred miles in the hot summer heat. Spending five weeks in the field, they followed Indian trails south to the Solomon River, then west, then north back to the Republican River, with no luck. Try as hard as they could, the soldiers could not gain ground on the elusive renegades. Scouting parties were sent out every day, but although they would run across the trail of a few horses, they were unable to find any lodge pole tracks that would indicate a moving village.

In the meantime, Tall Bull's Dog Soldiers had struck out from the Frenchman River across the Sandhills toward what is now North Platte, Nebraska. Finding the Platte River and other streams too full for a safe crossing, Tall Bull made the fatal mistake of going into camp on White Butte Creek, near today's Sterling, Colorado.

Confident that the soldiers could not find him, Tall Bull neglected to take any safety precautions. In fact, when the soldiers attacked, most of the warriors were lounging around their lodges oblivious to any danger.

It appears (as Nellie Snyder Yost writes in *Buffalo Bill, His Family, Friends, Fame, Failures, and Fortune*) that it was Cody who located the Cheyenne camp that July afternoon. Yost indicates this was confirmed by several members of the 5th Cavalry. One member named Leicester Walker wrote in his memoirs...

The trail was lost. No sign of any trail could be seen. General Carr ordered Cody to try to find the trail. He also ordered Major North to send some of his best scouts to locate the trail if possible. Six Pawnee scouts left the command going down the river. Cody went alone over to the hills to the west. In about an hour Cody returned to the command with the report he found the village, that it was about a half mile long and located near some springs. While Cody was reporting to the general, the Pawnee scouts returned, informing Carr they had found Indian sign.

Carr divided his command into three parts. Major W. Royall went with Cody on a right hand trail leading toward the northeast. The North Brothers and thirty five Pawnee scouts took the middle trail north, and Carr the right hand trail to the northwest. Luther North said later...

The weather was very hot and we could not travel very fast, but went on a slow trot most of the time. When he had gone fifteen miles, we were overtaken by one of the boys that we had sent with General Carr, with orders to join him at once, as they had discovered the Cheyenne village.

Preparations were made to attack the village and the entire command broke camp about two o'clock in the afternoon and headed towards the Cheyenne encampment three miles away. Traveling several miles, they came to a bluff overlooking a small valley. From there, they could clearly see the unsuspecting Cheyenne village sitting near the end of the valley floor.

The command rode within perhaps a mile and a half of the village, and would have crept much closer had it not been for a company on the right flank passing over a rise of ground and thus becoming exposed to the village. General Carr was informed of this fact, and being afraid that the company had been observed, he at once ordered the bugler to sound the charge. Instantly, the stirring notes of the bugle rang out clear and loud, and they charged the village.

The Cheyenne were lying in camp that day, and their war ponies grazed on the prairie a little distance from their lodges. There was no doubt the Cheyenne were completely surprised. It was a hot, humid day, and a great many were lounging in the shade of their lodges when the blue clad troopers rode into view.

The initial charge caused the Cheyenne to flee in panic, leaving everything behind them. Only a few were able to reach their ponies and many fled on foot. Some were able to escape while a large number dodged into ravines, little pockets, and washouts in the nearby hills.

When the fighting began, Tall Bull shot Mrs. Alderdice in the forehead—killing her instantly—and also shot Mrs. Weichel in the breast. When the Pawnees dashed up to the lodge, Mrs. Weichel thought the villages had been attacked by Indians hostile to the Cheyenne, and that she was about to escape from one band to fall captive at the hands of another.

The rout was complete. Never had the Cheyenne suffered such a devastating defeat. The result of the attack was the killing of fifty two warriors, and the capture of eighteen women and children. General Carr's official report listed 274 horses, 144 mules, 9,300 pound of dry meat, 56 rifles, 22 revolvers, 40 bows and arrows, 20 boxes of percussion caps, sabres, lances, and tomahawks. The soldiers also recovered scalps of white women and a necklace of human fingers.

The Cheyenne had an abundance of everything usually found in an Indian camp, besides a great number of articles which they had taken from the white settlers they had killed on the Saline River. Quite a large amount of gold and silver money was found by the soldiers. That night the command camped in the captured village, and late in the evening the supply wagon arrived.

The following morning, Mrs. Alderdice was buried on the battlefield. The burial service was read by one of the officers who was a religious man, as there was no chaplain in the command. General Carr gave the name of Susanna to the place where the battle occurred, that being Mrs. Alderdice's Christian name. The name was afterwards changed to Summit Springs because there was a spring of cool, clear water on a summit of a nearby sandhill where nobody supposed there was a drop of water. That same day, all the Indian lodges, buffalo robes, camp equipment, and dried buffalo meat were gathered together and burned by order of General Carr.

That afternoon, the command proceeded to Fort Sedgewick at Julesburg, Colorado, from where news of the fight was telegraphed to military headquarters. The Indian prisoners were sent to the Whetstone Agency on the Missouri River, and the captured horses and mules were distributed among the officers, soldiers, and scouts. Tall Bull and his followers had long been a terror to the border settlements, and resolutions in the Nebraska and Colorado State Legislatures were passed that winter commending General Carr and the Pawnee Scouts for their valuable service.

Who killed Tall Bull has remained controversial to this day, with credit being given to Buffalo Bill and Frank North. At the time, Buffalo Bill claimed credit for killing the renegade chief which in a sense, launched him on his colorful career. Of both claims, I'm convinced Frank North's claim to be the strongest.

Nellie Yost makes the point in her book, *Buffalo Bill,* that it was Cody who killed Tall Bull that hot July afternoon. She writes....

> Cody wrote that after the battle and while the Indian camp was being burned, some mounted Indians came charging back to rescue some of their possessions. One came charging through on a fine bay horse, exhorting the others to follow him and fight until they died. The bay horse attracted Cody's eye and he determined to have the animal. Hiding in the head of a ravine he waited until the Indian came by at closer range and shot him from the horse. Lt. George Mason jumped from his own horse and recovered the fallen Indian's warbonnet while Sgt. McGrath, who had seen Cody kill the rider, caught the horse and handed it over to him.

> I [Cody] rode the horse down to the place where the soldiers were holding their Indian prisoners. There, one of the women began crying in a pitiful and hysterical manner at sight of the horses, and upon inquiry, I found that she was Tall Bull's wife. She stated that this

123

was her husband's favorite war horse and that only a short time ago she had seen Tall Bull riding him.

However, Luther North saw it differently. He says...

We started up the hill out of the village on the west side. My brother (Frank) and I were a little ahead and to the left of our own men when an Indian who was hidden in a ravine stuck his head up and fired at my brother. At first I thought he was hit, as he threw his hand up and stopped his horse. He jumped off his horse and handed me his bridle reins and said, "Ride away and he will stick his head up again."

I started the horses off on a lope and the Indian raised his head to look, but did not get it very high, as my brother was ready for him and shot him in the forehead. His rifle remained on top of the bank, cocked and ready to fire. Later that day, Tall Bull was found lying directly under that spot.

Luther North (Nebraska State Historical Society)

124

I turned back and dismounted, and just then an Indian woman and little child climbed up from the ravine where the Indian had fallen back and came over to us. She knelt down before my brother and in sign language asked him to save her. Frank replied in similar language, telling her to go to the rear and remain there until he should call for her. She informed him that there were seven Indians alive in the ravine. The firing was kept kept up from the ravine for awhile, but finally ceased altogether. Frank and some of his men approached the ravine and looked over the bank. Down at the bottom they saw eighteen warriors lying dead.

The woman who approached my brother was Tall Bull's wife, and the Indian killed was Tall Bull himself, though we did not know it until we got back to Fort Sedgwick three days later when the interpreter, Leo Palliday, asked the woman if Tall Bull was killed. She said yes, pointing to my brother, "this man killed him when I came out of the canyon."

While Frank never cared whether or not he got credit for killing the infamous Cheyenne chief, Luther maintained until his dying day that Frank killed Tall Bull and not Buffalo Bill.

Ms. Yost stated that as Luther grew older, he became increasingly upset to see Cody's fame grow while his and Frank's accomplishments were all but forgotten. She felt that Luther embellished Frank's feats each time he was asked to tell about the old days.

I submit the following argument:

1. It's hard to believe that Tall Bull would have deliberately ridden back into the village which was swarming with soldiers just to retrieve some possessions.

2. I find it hard to believe Tall Bull would have left his wife and child at the mercy of the Pawnee to ride back into the village. For the most part, prisoners were not taken, especially by enemies that hated each other as much as the Pawnee and Cheyenne. Tall Bull knew the Pawnee would not have taken any prisoners.

3. It was widely known that Cody did not know the Indian language, yet he says he heard Tall Bull exhorting other warriors to follow him into camp and die for glory. How could this be?

4. In response to the statements written later by members of the 5th Calvary supporting Cody's claim, I believe the natural animosity the "regular" soldiers had toward the Pawnee Scouts and the North brothers led to their claiming that their own scout, Cody, killed Tall Bull.

5. Ms. Yost relied on Buffalo Bill's own statement as to who killed Tall Bull. Cody was a man who was noted for stretching the truth if it would benefit him.

6. It's true that the North brothers were overshadowed by Cody, but Luther gave credit to Cody for being a fine man and a great showman. Most importantly, the

North brothers were not generally known for lying.

7. Luther maintained from 1869 to his death in 1935 that Frank killed Tall Bull. He didn't start making the claim when he was an old man.

8. General Carr is quoted as saying that Tall Bull, "firing as he charged...[was killed] by Cody's unerring rifle fire..." and that when Cody led a horse into camp, "Mrs. Tall Bull said that was her husband's horse." The accuracy of Carr's statement is questionable in light of the statement in his official report that the chief "killed his own horse."

No matter what really happened that day, the power of the Cheyenne Dog Soldiers was broken, and the settlements could breathe easier.

Bibliography

A Withdrawal from the State Treasury

Koepke, Judy. "How Not To Rob the State Treasury." *Nebraskaland Magazine.* August 1968, pp. 25-27, 51.

The Lynching of Elizabeth Taylor

Creigh, Dorothy Weye. "Adams County—The People." Adams County Historical Society. 1972.

Hastings Gazette Journal. March 15, 16, 17, 1885.

Williams, Jean. "The Lynching of Elizabeth Taylor." The Press of The Territories—no date. Publication is on file at the Adams County Historical Society, Hastings, NE.

The Only Legal Hanging in Custer County

Custer County Museum. Custer, South Dakota.

Custer County Chronicle. June 1, 1939.

Kingsbury, George W. *History of Dakota Territory.* S.J. Clarke, 1915.

McClintock, John S. *Pioneer Days in the Black Hills.* J.J. Little and Ives, 1939.

Rapid City Journal. January 23, 1972.

Rapid City Journal. August 5, 1973.

State of South Dakota. Historical Collections. 1974.

The Committee of 33

Creigh, Dorothy Weye. "Adams County—The People." Adams County Historical Society, 1972.

"The Committee of 33." *Adams County Historical News.* Hastings, NE. September 1982.

The Lynching of Kid Wade

Buhn, Mina Clark. "The Story of Kid Wade." *Nebraska History Quarterly.* July-September 1933, p. 195.

Haugen, T. Josephine. "Kid Wade," *Nebraska History Quarterly,* January-March 1933, p. 18-34.

Hutton, Harold. *Doc Middleton.* Swallow Press: Chicago, IL, 1974.

Long Pine Journal. February 13, 1884.

Omaha World-Herald. February 9, 1884.

O'Neill Frontier. January 24, 1884.

O'Neill Frontier. February 2, 1884.

Yankton Press. January 19, 1884.

The Great Pawnee Defeat of 1873.

Shallenberger, A.C. "Massacre Canyon," *Nebraska History Quarterly,* July-September 1935, pp. 131-178.

The Battle of Ash Hollow

Hyde, George. *Spotted Tail's Folk: A History of the Brulé Sioux.* University of Oklahoma Press: Norman, OK.

"Reminiscences of the Indian Fight at Ash Hollow." Richard C. Drum, Collections of the Nebraska State Historical Society, Lincoln, NE.

Soldiers West. ed. Paul Andrew Hutton, University of Nebraska Press: Lincoln, NE, 1987.

"The Harney Expedition Against the Sioux: The Journal of Capt. John B.S. Todd." ed. Ray H. Mattison, *Nebraska History Quarterly,* 43, 1962.

Utley, Robert M. *Frontiersmen in Blue.* University of Nebraska Press: Lincoln, NE, 1967.

The Scalping of William Thompson

"Massacre at Plum Creek." *Nebraskaland Magazine.* June 1963.

How Philip Wells Lost His Nose

Eli S. Ricker Interviews, MS8 Box 4, Reel 1, Tablets 3, 4, 5. Nebraska State Historical Society. Lincoln, NE.

"The Wounded Knee Interviews of Eli S. Ricker. ed. Donald F. Danker." *Nebraska History Quarterly.* Vol. 62. Summer 1981. Nebraska State Historical Society, Lincoln, NE.

The Story of Dewey Beard

Eli S. Ricker Interviews, MS8 Box 6, Reel 5, Tablet 30. Nebraska State Historical Society. Lincoln, NE.

"The Wounded Knee Interviews of Eli S. Ricker. ed. Donald F. Danker." *Nebraska History Quarterly.* Vol. 62. Summer 1981. Nebraska State Historical Society, Lincoln, NE.

The Nat and Robert Martin Story

Hastings Daily Tribune. October 21, 1921.

Martin Post Office. File kept at the Adams County Historical Society. Hastings, NE.

Who Killed Tall Bull?

Danker, Donald. "The North Brothers." *Nebraska History Quarterly.*
September 1931. pp. 161-70.
King, James T. "The Republican River Expedition June-July 1869."
Nebraska History Quarterly. September 1960. pp. 165-204.
King, James T. "The Republican River Expedition June-July 1869."
Nebraska History Quarterly. December 1960. pp. 281-300.
North, Luther. *Man of the Plains.* ed. Donald Danker. University of
Nebraska Press, 1961.
Sheldon, A.E. "Frank North." *Nebraska History Quarterly.*
July-September 1932. p. 136.
Sheldon, A.E. "Frank North." *Nebraska History Quarterly.*
October-December 1934. pp. 260-76.
Yost, Nellie Snyder. *Buffalo Bill.* Swallow Press: Chicago, IL, 1979.

Index